The Glance of the Medusa

THE HUNGARIAN LIST

THE HUNGARIAN LIST
Series Editor
Ottilie Mulzet

LÁSZLÓ F. FÖLDÉNYI

The Glance of the Medusa

The Physiognomy of Mysticism

TRANSLATED BY JOZEFINA KOMPORALY

LONDON NEW YORK CALCUTTA

Seagull Books, 2020

Second printing, 2021

© László F. Földényi, 2020
English translation © Jozefina Komporaly, 2020

All images sourced from the public domain

Quotation from *Four Quartets* by T. S. Eliot reproduced with kind permission
from Faber and Faber Ltd, UK

ISBN   978 0 8574 2 608 6

British Library Cataloguing-in-Publication Data
A catalogue record for this book is available from the British Library

Typeset by Seagull Books, Calcutta, India
Printed and bound by WordsWorth India, New Delhi, India

CONTENTS

MOTTOS

'... [U]ltimately one experiences only oneself. The time has passed in which accidents *could* still befall me, and what could fall to me now that is not already my own? It merely returns, it finally comes home to me—my own self and everything in it that has long been abroad and scattered among all things and accident [...] Peak and abyss—they are now merged as one! [...] You go your own way of greatness; here no one shall sneak along after you! Your foot itself erased the path behind you, and above it stands written: impossibility.' (Friedrich Nietzsche)

'The fire of the gods drives us to set forth by day
And by night. So come, let us look at what is apparent.'
(Friedrich Hölderlin)

'The body is capable of a degree of tension, fragmentation, density, and impenetrability that surpasses all philosophy, dialectics, music, physics, poetry, and magic', Antonin Artaud contended shortly before his death in his lecture 'Theatre and Science'. Seeing his audience's seeming incomprehension, he added: 'I would have had to shit blood through my navel in order to make myself understood and to arrive at what I wanted.'

'God isn't humanity's limit-point, though humanity's limit-point is divine. Or put it this way—humanity is divine when experiencing limits.' (Georges Bataille)

'That there was a Deluge once, seems not to mee so great a miracle, as that there is not one alwayes.' (Sir Thomas Browne)

'[D]eath is not the pathos of the ultimate human possibility, the possibility of impossibility, but the ceaseless repetition of what cannot be grasped, before which the *I* loses its ipseity. The impossibility of possibility [. . .] In death [. . .] the regular order is reversed, since, in it, power leads to what is unassumable. Thus the distance between life and death is infinite [. . .] Death is not the end, it is the never-ending ending.' (Emmanuel Levinas)

'Time present and time past
Are both perhaps present in time future
And time future contained in time past.'
(T. S. Eliot)

INTRODUCTION

'God creates out of nothing, man out of ruins. We must break our-selves to pieces before we know what we are, what we can be and do!' (*Don Juan and Faust* 1.2) Romantic playwright Christian Dietrich Grabbe wrote these lines for one of the protagonists of his 1829 tragedy. As is his custom, Faust aims high. He wishes to accomplish what allegedly is God's due, on his own. For this, how-ever, he needs to defy God himself. He attempts creation, too. His circumstances and possibilities are radically different from those of a supposed God though. God created Something out of Nothing; Faust, however, can only create Something new from something already existing. In order for this Something to be as final and sub-stantial as God's creation, it needs to actually rise above and super-sede the Something created by God. But since God is supreme, meaning that he is above all, this 'supersedure' can only bear fruit if done in the opposite direction. God needs to be 'eclipsed' in order for Faust to supersede him. As Heinrich von Kleist outlined in his study on marionette theatre (1810), written just prior to Grabbe's play: '[W]e would have to eat once more of the tree of knowledge in order to fall back into the state of innocence [. . .] Yes, [. . .] that is the final chapter in the history of the world' (2013: 47).

To eclipse God means to ignore his work, that is, creation, and in parallel, to also ignore what preceded creation, that is, Nothing-ness. While on a path to self-destruction, Grabbe's hero also attempts a spiritual adventure. God created a world out of Nothing-ness: essentially claiming that all there is (the World, Something, the Existent/Be-ing) has been preceded by whatever cannot be called the World, Something or the Existent/Be-ing, and for this reason it is, by definition, also greater than these. Could this be

anything other than Nothingness, or—in Heidegger's terms—
Being? The creative act attributed to God draws attention to the
most fundamental tradition of European thought, metaphysical
thought, the theological character of which had been pinpointed
by Heidegger:

> Ever since being got interpreted as ιδεα, thinking about the
> being of beings has been metaphysical, and metaphysics
> has been theological. In this case theology means the inter-
> pretation of the "cause" of beings as God and the transfer-
> ring of being onto this cause, which contains being in itself
> and dispenses being from out of itself, because it is the
> being-est of beings (1998b: 181).

Grabbe's Faust aims for no less at the beginning of the nineteenth century than to bid farewell to this metaphysical tradition
that goes back over two thousand years. At the same time, he also
wants to bid farewell to an idea that has stubbornly entrenched itself
in European thought: namely, that Nothingness, because it precedes
everything, is richer than the Something created thereof. Faust does
not believe in Nothingness, but he does believe in creation. And
with this, he initiates a new tradition, which has consolidated into
an increasingly strong influence ever since the Romantic Age, and,
by the beginning of the third millennium, has gained a credibility
in political thinking akin to the one enjoyed by the metaphysical
disposition two thousand years ago. This new tradition aims to
bridge the abyss between Being and Be-ing, and to do away with the
difference between the two. Faust's plan is, to use a modern term,
the deconstruction of simple, traditional metaphysical thinking.
To create from rubble or to turn ourselves into rubble—in order to
find out who and what we are—is the rejection of the idea of
Nothingness as a precedent to everything, a renunciation of the
belief that sooner or later one can reach a final—or initial—handle,
the certitude of the Whole and the Complete, which shines like a
sun illuminating everything that follows (or precedes) it.

Traditional metaphysics is underpinned by a belief in a supposedly final and positive meaning, which meaning, by virtue of its very nature, also differentiates itself from everything that it invests with meaning. This traditional understanding of meaning, the abyss between Being and Be-ing, entices us with the prospect of a new world that, although available to all, can only be accessed if one renounces everything there is, and abandons what appears to be without meaning. But why does this appear enticing? Because all that there is, in other words, Be-ing , creates the impression of a compulsion that prevents people from achieving precisely what Grabbe's Faust is also craving: to find out who they are and what they are capable of.

In lieu of an earthly, and hence fractured, Self-image, metaphysical thinking is fascinated by a solid and definitive, hence divine, Self-image, which allegedly awaits us somewhere, however hard it may be to find. Grabbe's Faust challenges the existence of such an essential Self-image. Available for everyone to identify with, it has constituted one of the pillars of European civilization for centuries. From the Romantic Age onwards, however, the inner cracks in metaphysical thinking have become increasingly visible. These cracks first appeared with the shaking of the belief in the traditional God-image. In parallel with the latter, the so-called divine Self-image had also become subject to interrogation, to the extent that in the mid-twentieth century, Czeslaw Miłosz could posit the following: 'The individual, proudly pointing to himself as "I", proved just as much an illusion, a bundle of reflexes covered by a uniform epidermis' (1985: 240).

Yet if the self is held together by an epidermis of sorts, is it then even possible to talk about any kind of 'inner' identity? This is a valid question because Grabbe's Faust—for simplicity's sake, let us dwell on this figure—does not give up his quest for self-discovery, despite rejecting the traditional essentialist Self-image. Moreover—anticipating Nietzsche—he would like to be in charge of creating his own self in the process of getting to know himself. He turns his back on metaphysical thinking, and at the same time refuses to reduce himself to dermal tissue—he does not wish to surrender to a school of thought that, at the end of the twentieth century, could be classed as pragmatic. According to pragmatism, any vain desire for 'inner identity' betrays a nostalgic quest for metaphysics. Richard Rorty noted that Freud helped us to 'see ourselves as center-less, as random assemblages of contingent and idiosyncratic needs rather than as more or less adequate exemplifications of a common human essence [. . .] This has been an important factor in our ability to slough off the idea that we have a true self, one shared with all other humans' (1991: 155).

By contrast, Faust—similar to this author—holds a different view. He does not challenge the fact that traditional metaphysical thinking has lost its general validity, meaning that it gave voice, long before Freud, to the hypothesis that the Self is no longer the master of his own house. On the other hand, he does not stop here. He does not accept the claim that the 'house' is empty, and takes his quest further. It is perhaps possible to come across the stranger who occupied the house. Faust pulls down the house, turns every-thing into rubble to find this stranger who is almost indistinguish-able from his own Self, yet who is infinitely distant and different from him. *He rejects the reign (terror) of a common and essential Self, yet he does not place individuality at the mercy of the machina-tions of probability and chance.* He does not argue against the 'self' being a mere illusion with untraceable boundaries, or being barely different from a mass of shapes and patterns, which, in response to current interests and situations, assemble into constantly changing configurations. At the same time, he also accepts the validity of another, barely compatible, matrix, and insists on the unity of iden-tity which cannot be reduced to the Self. In his view, individuality is simultaneously solid and flexible, and, despite having a single facet, it cannot be looked in the eye. In other words—referencing frequently used terminology in European culture—individuality is the endless reflection of mirrors reflecting one another, while, above all, actually reflecting the divine.

This 'divine' lurks behind the positive 'God' fashioned by traditional religions, and transcends the former by succumbing. A mere century after Grabbe, at the turn of the nineteenth century, Alfred Jarry wrote in his preface to *Ubu in Chains*: 'Hornsboodle, we should never have knocked everything down if we hadn't meant to destroy the ruins, too. But the only way we see of doing that is to put up some handsome buildings' (quoted in Shattuck 1968: 226). Nihilism gives rise to a new individuality—and the dismantling of traditional metaphysics opens up new horizons for a new, dynamic metaphysics. Over the last two centuries, European culture has lost its metaphysical connections. Mankind, however, as Leszek Kołakowski posited in his book *Metaphysical Horror* (1988), can never liberate itself from the desire for transcendence and metaphysics. Human beings are doomed to metaphysics owing to their awareness of their own mortality, if for no other reason. Faust maintains his attraction to traditional metaphysics; at the same time, he does not allow himself to be locked into prisons erected in its name. This author follows his example. The forthcoming seven essays replicate the attempt of Grabbe's protagonist: to construct and deconstruct at the same time. Each of the seven chapters addresses a different topic (where the bars of the cross intersect, lightning, the centre, crossing boundaries, chaos, the impossible, and the oppressive power of now), yet they are all channelled towards the same invisible focus.

Grabbe's protagonist refers to God, not only because he has to defy him with reference to creation but also because metaphysical thinking is unavoidably overshadowed by the figure (concept) of God. It is difficult to steer clear of him—even for those who, like this author, do not consider themselves believers and are not in pursuit of solace rooted in religion. Yet, I use the term 'religion', or, rather, 'religious', generously in my book, in the sense attributed to the term by Hungarian thinker Béla Hamvas. Hamvas once made the following point: I am not religious yet the most defining moments of my life were religious experiences. I consider as religious those experiences that help people overcome their inner, hitherto-insurmountable barriers. This has very little to do with belief, and canonized religion can definitely not be moulded from it. In the throes of religious experience, Man feels boundless and limitless. This experience could be classed as cathartic, moving or uplifting. Summed up in a single word: mystical, or, better still, ecstatic. Mystical experiences are ecstatic because they make one transcend oneself and one's so-called natural habitat, and open up horizons that re-situate existence in a new light. Moreover, they make one aware that one 'exists'. To be precise, they draw attention to the fact that one does exist, although it would be equally self-evident not to exist. Religions try to protect one from losing oneself. By contrast, mystical experiences feed on 'loss' and it is this that they transform into gain. In the throes of mystical experience, one finds oneself in a state of such unexpected and unprecedented coherence as if encountering one's identity for the first time. Meanwhile, one also feels forsaken: the transcendence of the self interrogates the very sense of identity. For this reason, such experiences are paradoxical: one achieves ipseity at the very point when this union is the least fathomable. Such experiences reveal the contradictory nature of human life: one is the least in charge over the single thing that is the utmost proof of existence—one's own life.

'It is only in inspired terms that the divine can be spoken of' (Hegel 1961: 255). The same can be said of religious experiences—with the significant proviso that the 'religious' (enthusiastic, ecstatic) tone needs to be extremely clear. The aim of this book is to circumscribe the touchstones of religious experience. But in order not to jeopardize this experience, and for it not to become too 'prosaic', every now and then one has to feel a little dizzy yet still hang on to common sense, and to be intrusive yet maintain critical distance. The aim is to suggest the unthinkable surrounding thought and the unspeakable concealed beyond speech. The essay as a genre offers itself as an ideal solution, since the original meaning of the word is none other than attempt. Essays are attempts at the impossible: they conjure up the same boundlessness that emerges in the course of religious experiences. Essays are credible not only because they pulsate with life but also because they emanate a sense of threat. In an essay, a single fire-ball-like moment spreads across time. It is this very deliberate contradiction inherent in the process of writing that ensures the unity of the forthcoming experience. Essays are attempts indeed, but they could not be carried out without the essayists themselves being haunted by their inner concerns. Essayists immerse themselves in (or put up with) their subject matter while nevertheless holding on to their freedom. The need for writing essays emerges when the topic has a personal dimension. Yet in this case, personal touches are an indication of temptation, which, to return to the previous idea, gives rise to an experience that also blurs the boundaries of individuality.

There is something awe-inspiring about religious experiences. Essays, by definition, are tempting by virtue of their ability to transmit this sense of astonishment, and it is this that makes me consider the history of culture not as a repository of data and events but as a vortex in which no single aspect is more prominent than any of the others. 'We are afraid of everything' [. . .], from the time we're born to the time we die [. . .] we're just plain terrified'—Louis-Ferdinand Céline wrote in his play *The Church*—'So that gets us thinking, it makes us study Science [. . .] as they call it. The most intelligent people are the ones who are the most frightened' (2003: 97). Science serves the purpose of concealing this fear. Footnotes, allusions and frequent citations serve this same purpose in the present book. There is a danger that in lieu of a vortex, they involuntarily fall into a system, held together by subordination and superordination. My aim with this is not to accuse, demonstrate or defend, but to illustrate that the present thoughts are oriented at phenomena that have already been experienced by others across cultures and historical moments. Calling upon figures from Heraclitus to Bataille, and from Basilides to Cioran, my aim is not to simply cite daunting icons and authorities but also to present them as my contemporaries of sorts. My intention is not to hammer in references and citations, though I am attracted to positivist philology and its extensive toolkit. If anything, I am looking for role models, such as the seventeenth-century English Baroque thinkers Robert Burton and Thomas Browne. Akin to their latter-day successor Jorge Luis Borges, they did not perceive the history of culture as a solvable puzzle but as a labyrinth, in which everyone is faced with the challenge of taking on board more or less the same questions.

CHAPTER 1

DIVINE EXPERIENCE AND DIVINE FAITH
(WHERE THE BARS OF THE CROSS INTERSECT)

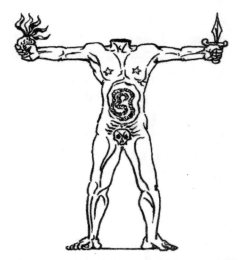

André Masson's cover for the first issue of *Acéphale* (1936)

The whole body pales; life attempts to depart along the trail of a single line. It cracks open as if lightning had torn it in two; one tries to escape from life like a creeping insect, vesting all hopes into something that can no longer be called life. But isn't one's sense of identity the strongest when one is particularly dispossessed? And isn't one the weightiest when one's selfhood can only be captured in its ever-transient imprint?

Limbs no longer move; the tongue retracts into the darkness of the echoing mouth cavity. The apple of the eye reflects a sense of the impossible. The blood-stripe running along the midline is the sign of an inner cross that bursts the body open. Life stretches upon its own cross. Are we about to witness the mystery of annihilating fulfilment?

[. . . U]ltimately one experiences only oneself. The time has passed in which accidents could still befall me, and what could fall to me now that is not already my own? It merely returns, it finally comes home to me—my own self and everything in it that has long been abroad and scattered among all things and accident [. . .]. Peak and abyss—they are now merged as one! [. . .] You go your own way of greatness; here no one shall sneak along after you! Your foot itself erased the path behind you, and above it stands written: impossibility.

Friedrich Nietzsche (2006: 121)

'Yet unto me there then appeared this yet more wonderful thing'— the author of the apocryphal Acts of John notes about Jesus—'for I would try to see him privily, and I never at any time saw his eyes closing, but only open' (1983[1924]: 251). This was not the only thing that struck him. In addition to keeping his eyes continuously open, Jesus had many other extraordinary qualities. Subsequently, he appeared as a child and then as a very old man; sometimes he stepped out as a giant, other times as a dwarf. He mostly had a physical body but he would also become entirely transfigured; looking either like himself or suddenly doubling up; he generally appeared as Jesus but, on occasion, he also blended into John. Thus, it is no wonder that *this* Jesus did not put a high price on persuasion, the method of rational argumentation. Prior to his capture, he burst into song and started dancing, inviting his disciples to join him. In the course of the dance, he fell into ecstasy, and in this way, made it possible for those standing and dancing around him to become privy to an unspeakable and undecipherable secret. Later he claimed that this dance was in the honour of the Father, and he interpreted it as a form of suffering. But why did he suffer? He does not reveal his reasons but feels that he has to keep silent about this suffering and says to John: 'but what I am I alone know, and no man else. Suffer me then to keep that which is mine, and that which is thine behold thou through me [. . .]. Thou hearest that I suffered, yet did I not suffer; that I suffered not, yet did I suffer' (ibid.: 256).

Emptying, Charging

'All mine are yours, and yours are mine' (John : 10). What could Jesus be possibly thinking? Oddly enough, although he does not let himself be seen, he calls upon John to gaze at him. John has to stare into the eye of the never-blinking Jesus. He has to keep staring until his eyes play him false. At this point it is no longer Jesus that he sees, and it would be difficult to decide what it is exactly that he can see. Perhaps he recognizes himself in his features. But it is also possible that everything starts spinning in front of his eyes, and he gets dizzy. Irrespective of what really happens, Logos—the embodiment of which Jesus claims to be, and which is stared in the face by John—is not suitable for being unpacked and revealed layer by layer. It does not even allow to be understood, and the rules of hermeneutics, when applied to this case, end in failure. This Jesus and this Logos are not the Jesus and Logos of theologians and philosophers; they are separated by an abyss from those who want to get to know them.

The Jesus of the Acts of John tempts John. He offers himself to John, creates the impression that he allows himself to be seen, yet he conceals himself and in the end, John stares at him in vain. He pretends to be tangible yet, in fact, he hides himself away, into John. He who wants to get to know him has to get to know his own self first—and catch the incoming stranger in the act. This Jesus is just like a psychotherapist: he aids those watching him to achieve self-knowledge. He lends 'substance' to others by revealing his own sense of void. Of course, he is also leading John by the nose a little. Had John been asked, he would have probably said that he is not led by anyone. Yet he is dazed, dizzy, and the world starts spinning around him as he stares at the never-blinking Jesus.

This Jesus offers fulfilment to John by simultaneously fuelling a sense of loss in him. He promises self-knowledge ('and yours are mine'), yet he also rejects John. Up until he actually had to face Jesus, John most probably saw him as an administrator of sorts. Like most believers, he was also hoping for the settling of his affairs. He thought of Jesus as of someone who was way ahead of him in every respect. God's often-mentioned intangibility made him think that Jesus was much more capable than ordinary people, he would wear a magic cap to make himself invisible and hence not allow to be seen by others for some reason. Yet now, when confronting this strange but humanly Jesus, he is forced to acknowledge that the phrase 'turn to God' is linguistically impossible. It is a useless metaphor. The thought of 'turning to God', in fact of the very term 'God', can only come to the fore when people feel that they can communicate their circumstances. In such situations, they are surrounded by peers, in other words, they live in society, one lynchpin of which is God (religion, *religio*) itself. The term ('God') appears to be truly meaningful in such cases, to the extent that it can be institutionalized and is even suitable to lay the foundations of the Church.

In the course of experiences such as the one John partook in, words are devoid of meaning. To be precise, they gain new content—content that is capable of suggesting the loss John felt when staring at the never-blinking Jesus. John got dizzy, the world ('society') lost its boundaries, yet his soul grew large. It grew so large that it was able to gobble up the entire world. John partook in a very particular experience: he found himself by losing the familiar world, and in exchange, he was granted a brand-new one. The term 'God' did not come to nothing but turned out of itself: it remained clear and intelligible while creating the impression of a dark tunnel. Similarly, the Acts of John is creating the impression that language is undermined and can blow up any minute.

'And yours are mine.' John partook in an experience that, according to European tradition, tends to be called mystical. Jesus turned John away from the God of institutions and habits, and confronted him with the fact that God can only be reserved 'one' place: the fracture that occurs within the self when one's very identity is under interrogation. John recognizes in the never-blinking Jesus his own self, although the features of the former are obviously different from his own. John is looking for what is his in the other or, to put it differently, he is approaching his self via the roundabout ways of a relative stranger. His 'self' is charged with content that is not directly connected to this 'self'.

This adventure of John, however, offers another lesson. This case illustrates that the point is not that there is an 'I' that precedes everything and which then starts to charge like a battery, but that this 'I' comes into being precisely by being charged with something that, strictly speaking, is no part thereof. 'I saw myself seeing myself': this claim reminiscent of the Acts of John is discussed two thousand years later by Jacques Lacan in *The Four Fundamental Concepts of Psycho-analysis*, where he analyses the foundations of consciousness (1978: 80). For Lacan, consciousness is inseparable from self-knowledge. Self-knowledge, however, cannot be restricted to consciousness. It is much more than that. A hundred years before Lacan, Nietzsche considered self-knowledge a form of self-creation, claiming that personality gives rise to itself at the same time as getting to know itself.

Jesus deliberately puts John at the crossroads while making the latter stare at him. In the past, John presumably thought of God as of someone who overtakes and supersedes him. This essentialist God-concept is accompanied by a self-image that is also potentially essentialist. While observing the never-blinking Jesus, however,

John partook in a radically different experience. God does not over-take him; rather, he starts to emerge in him, just like his self only starts to take shape now, in the course of distancing himself from his former self. To utilize a deliberately paradoxical image: the greater (God) is manifested in the lesser (John), the complete in the incomplete. John is at the crossroads between moderation and excess. He either accepts moderation as an exclusive norm—and then ignores the fact that the very basis of moderation is something that, strictly speaking, cannot be measured; or he says yes to excess which, in this case, does not lead to chaos and anarchy but to the paradoxical unity of moderation and excess. He either excludes or accepts.

Those who, like John, have the opportunity to look Jesus in the eye and feel that God is nascent in them, turn to privatives as a result of the paradoxical association between moderation and excess. They are, without fail, the stylists of negative theology, from Origenes to Simone Weil, Plotinus to Georges Bataille, Meister Eckhart to E. M. Cioran, notwithstanding the Gnostics and mystics. Teachings on the intangibility of God are either poetic expressions or affirmations, enshrouded in theology, of this very paradox. The cause of this unavoidable obscurity in the case of Gnostics and mys-tics is not a lack of precision in formulating ideas but the fact that language is oriented at an object, and this orientation is part and parcel of linguistic formulation itself. Aided by words, they are trying to circumscribe phenomena that they already possess, and are chasing something that already lags behind. A good example in this sense is the almost comically obstinate endeavour of second-century Gnostic Basilides, to convey the relationship between 'being above being (existence)' and 'non-being' in terms of ridiculing terminology:

> There was when naught was; nay, even that 'naught' was
> not aught of things that are (even in the world of reality).
> But nakedly, conjecture and mental quibbling apart, there

was absolutely not even the One [. . .] Naught was, neither matter, nor substance, nor voidness of substance, nor simplicity, nor impossibility-of-composition, nor inconceptibility, nor imperceptibility, neither man, nor angel, nor god; [. . .] Such, or rather far more removed from the power of man's comprehension, was the state of non-being, when the Deity beyond being, without thinking, or feeling, or determining, or choosing, or being compelled, or desiring, willed to create universality. When I use the term 'will', I do so merely to suggest the idea of an operation transcending all volition, thought or sensible action [. . .]. Thus the Divinity beyond being created universality beyond being from elements beyond being (Mead 1906: 256–8).

We can only do justice to Basilides if we do not even attempt to translate his words into the language of reason. A 'translated' version of the quote would read as follows: 'In the beginning God created the heavens and the earth.' (The first line of the Bible satisfies the criterion of reason, but only on the face of it. This sentence is particularly fragile. The thought of the beyond the imaginable, of 'being above existence', and its antonym 'Nothingness' are dormant therein.) Basilides is not attempting to retell the story of creation but to convey an experience akin to John's while observing the never-blinking Jesus. Basilides tries to transpose a mythical creation story into the language of personal experience and, in the process, locates personal experience into a mythical framework. These days we would formulate this experience in the following way: everything that there is did not exist before; in other words, everything that has come into being owes its nascence to something that is not of the same ilk. Basilides does not claim anything less than that the ultimate raw material for existence in constant creation is something that is non-existent. Using the language of negative theology: the utmost proof of God's existence is his very non-existence.

It is hard to ignore the fact that Basilides' complex argument is rooted in a sense of dissatisfaction with existence. He must have experienced a profound sense of lack in order to arrive at such claims. The origin of this lack is a rupture that he must have experienced between the self and the world. Yet he could only amplify this experience to a mythical level by avoiding to preface this sense of lack with a negative note. Instead, he recognized its potential and saw it as a source of energy. And as if with a magic touch, the original sense of deprivation transformed into recharging. All of a sudden, the lack experienced in existence turned into fulfilment. We are talking not about a gradual transformation here but about a genuine catastrophe in the original sense of the word—'a Damascean conversion'. In the European tradition, this is called enlightenment, 'conversion', repentance (see Macho 1993: 491)—terms that constitute the very basis of all mystical experiences.

The 'personal encounter with God', known as the key characteristic of mysticism, is the seemingly moderate expression to convey the experience of mystics who have simultaneously lived a given moment (the moment of 'conversion') as deprivation and excessive fulfilment. The power of Basilides' words does not reside in the theological or ontological truth they carry but in their transmission of this experience. Reading his apocrypha, it appears as if it was he who probably first formulated the famous Heideggerian question: 'Why are there beings at all, and why not rather nothing?' (1998d: 96)

Moments of Approaching God

When in the course of his pilgrimages, Apollonius of Tyana, a first-century preacher, encountered Wisdom (Sophia), the latter said the following to the pagan man who was more respected for his teachings and miracles than Christ himself, and who was later successfully erased from the memory of organized religion: 'And when you are pure I will grant you the faculty of foreknowledge, and I will so fill your eyes with light, that you shall distinguish a god, and recognize a hero, and detect and put to shame the shadowy phantoms which disguise themselves in the form of men' (Philostratus, *The Life of Apollonius of Tyana* 6.11). She declared wisdom and cleansing as fundamental conditions for catching a glimpse of the divine. But what should one be cleansed of? Apollonius set out the conditions for cleanliness in the following statement: '[H]e should sacrifice (for the deity) nothing at all, neither kindle fire, nor dedicate anything that is an object of sense' (Eusebius of Caesarea, *Praeparatio Evangelica* 4.13). Thus, one has to leave the world of the senses in order to access the world of the divine. Approaching the latter, however, one does not only leave the world of the senses behind but also moderation. It was in fact Apollonius who stated that only the world (cosmos) has a sense of moderation (ibid.: 8.7). One can only experience cleansing if, in the course of approaching the divine, one also leaves behind the world of moderation. Thus the preacher of Tyana claims that one can only approach God if lending oneself over to a vortex that ousts oneself from one's very own self. In other words, this is only possible if one experiences life not as an ensemble of transitions, roads and bridges but as an insurmountable abyss.

It was the promise of glancing at the Gods that Wisdom promised to Apollonius. A few centuries earlier, however, Socrates tried to persuade everyone to love wisdom—philosophy, that is—because it is only thus that they can prepare to face death. In parallel with cunningly beguiling Apollonius with the promise of glancing at the gods, Wisdom was in fact trying to persuade him that in the vicinity of gods he will realize that the raw material of existence is something that does not really exist, and which cannot be described as 'that' but, rather—defying the rules of language— as 'that, that isn't that'. This is the most important experience in store for Apollonius. He will not be taught this by the gods but, rather, if he experiences this lack residing in existence, he can then get closer to the gods—and God will be nascent in him. This 'one-person God' is the God of absence; it is his duty, as Socrates indicated, to prepare Man for death.

Divine Experience and Divine Faith

Those initiated into the Mithras mystery, intended as a preparation for immortality, were in pursuit of similar experiences to the one that Jesus offered to John gazing at him in the Acts of John. They also craved for the sight of gods looking at them. They held the belief that if their glance were to meet that of the gods, then the soul would not only depart from its self but also enter some other place.

According to this view, sight is a condition of initiation. To be precise, this is the kind of sight that does not look at something specific but turns back upon itself. Mystics identified in the gaze immersing in itself the very sign of having found God. This must have been at the forefront of the Irish Scotus Erigena's mind, when he wrote in the ninth century that sight is no different from Being (see Schmitt 1903: 2.96). Divine experience is manifested via enhanced sight (accompanied by heightened hearing and touch). Oddly enough though, it is during the very process of approaching God that God's invisibility, immortality and intangibility gain experiential qualities. Tacitus noted about the Germanic tribes that 'they give divine names to that mysterious something which is visible only to the eyes of faith' (Tacitus, *Germania* 9.3). Paradoxically, in the throes of divine experience, the object of sensorial contact is something that cannot actually be experienced. In such situations, we become aware that there is Nothing to see, and hear that there is Nothing to hear. 'I have nothing to say and I'm saying it,' John Cage wrote in 'Lecture on Nothing' (1973: 109). Mystics would put this in the following way: I cannot see God, yet I see God; I cannot hear God, yet I hear God.

This is the point where 'divine experience' and 'divine faith' part company. In the course of divine experience, what cannot be experienced becomes the subject of experience—excess appears within the parameters of moderation—while divine faith separates knowledge and experience, and differentiates moderation from excess. The former confronts humans with the infinite while not removing the weight of finitude from their shoulders; the latter, by contrast, seems to lessen the weight (by not conceptualizing it as an ultimate annihilation) of finitude (mortality). Divine experience is intense, heated, momentary, and it makes no allowance for past or future, since it makes no allowance for time either. Utter aimlessness is as much a characteristic of these moments as ultimate fulfilment. This is why such moments can be considered sacred. Understandably, viewed from the perspective of divine faith, the notion of divine experience is rather suspect. This is why, in various cultures, the sacred could mean not only purity but also pollution. The Greek term *hagios* and the Latin *sacer* referred not only to the sacred but also to damnation (see Harrison 1957: 59; Eliade 1978: 37), and this is typical for Arabic, Hebrew and Egyptian usage too (Albright 1957: 176). This proves that, after all, divine experience is incompatible with moderation: in the course of divine experience, Man benefits from the sanctity of anarchy. In other words, it demonstrates openness despite not knowing what to expect. This is a state of freedom, a fountain of possibilities, without the ability to figure out what shape freedom will adopt in the end.

By contrast, divine faith can be exercised in moderation. This is why the former is suitable for institutional organization, unlike divine experience. It goes without saying that divine faith fails just as much as divine experience when trying to convincingly clarify the problem of death and mortality; but instead of fully (that is, excessively) experiencing this obvious and tragic contradiction of existence, it suppresses both the possibility of despair and the experience of being completely lost.

Involved in debates with the Gnostics, the early fathers of the Church went out of their way to institute a reassuring image of the divine. An anonymous third-century Gnostic text mentions the prophet Phosilampes, who, having realized that the essence of the universe resides in the indescribable, unspeakable and invincible, the divinity of which cannot be described by someone who is not also a divine being, noted: 'Those things which verily and truly exist and those which do not truly exist are for his sake. This is he for whose sake are those that truly exist which are secret, and those that do not truly exist which are manifest' (*The Books of Jeu* 1978: 237). The difference between divine experience and divine faith can be easily illuminated if we contrast this with the contention of Irenaeus, who, in his debates with the Gnostics, stated that the notion of an unknown God is not the same as the original chaos (*buthos*) as suggested by the Gnostics, since the former is the creator of the world, the invisible father: God, 'as regards His greatness, is indeed unknown to all [. . .]; but as regards His love, He is always known through Him by whose means He ordained all things' (Irenaeus of Lyons, *Against Heresies* 4.20.4, quoted in Norden 1913: 75). The Gnostics have expanded the fate of the abandoned soul to universal dimensions; by contrast, the fathers of the Church emphasized the role of religion in community formation and preservation.

The Balance of Irresolvable Chaos

Our sense of being at the mercy of the world and of circumstances appears to be self-evident to such an extent that we barely register it. The actual meaning of this, however, only emerges in the course of divine experience. On the one hand, the individual experiences the sentiment that it is no longer captive to the world, space or time. On the other hand, the authenticity of the earlier vulnerability is also illuminated. To be precise, this phenomenon sheds light on the fact that what one perceived as defencelessness was not a mere dependence on the world and on circumstances but a whole lot more. In this situation, moderation contains the seeds of excess, and it turns out that everything that surrounds the individual, and exists, is also a guise of the chaos that overrides existence. In the throes of divine experience, one feels free because one does not depend on this guise any longer; however, one soon finds oneself in a new situation of dependency—as one feels dependant on the chaos that cannot be subjugated by any means whatsover.

Starting from Plato, via the Neoplatonians and all the way to Christianity, it is possible to trace a process whereby there are attempts to tame universal chaos and to stylize it into an all-reconciliatory Unity. This could just as well be called Unity beyond existence as it could be called God; and—according to Plato—this fails to partake in a share of existence to such a degree that it should in fact be called Non-existing Unity (*Parmenides* 163d). It is easier to postulate and state paradigms and ideas than ultimate causes, as the fifth-century Neoplatonian Damascius contends in his explication of Plato's *Phaedo*: 'The latter is truly ineffable and is beyond having visible images (no image of it exists); moreover, in the world of process it disappears because of the indefiniteness which is inherent in process and which causes all the evil that pervades it' (Westerink 1977: 416).

The Neoplatonians handled the question of divine intangibility in a much more risk-taking way than the Christians; but they also held back from bringing tragedies, rifts, irresolvable paradoxes, though part and parcel of life, into contact with divine Unity. They also felt reluctant to presuppose an intimate relationship between existence and the so-called Unity beyond existence, because this would have drawn attention to the points of contact between this Unity and chaos itself. According to Plotinus, we are unable to form an opinion of Unity because mind and speech can be categorized by multiplicity (we can only touch what belongs to the rank of objects) and are manifold. There is no speech (*logos*), sense (*aisthesis*) and knowledge (*episteme*) about Unity (see Plotinus, *Enneads* 5.8.11). A precondition of cognition is a sense of doing away with the world, which he calls abstraction (*aphaeresis*). Yet, in this process of abstraction from the world, he only wishes to notice fulfilment and upliftment, although the latter also involves the danger of the fall. The foundation of experiential, and hence not only conceptual, abstraction is vision. But since vision relates to the sighting of the nascent God in the human being, it brings life to light in the magic mirror of decay.

Clement of Alexandria (at the turn of the second and third centuries) also sees fulfilled abstraction as a precondition for the sighting of God (in his view, mind has to practise to deprive the material body of its physical qualities, such as depth, width, length and, finally, place). And despite the fact that he states, using a Platonian term, that the mind does not learn at this point what he (the Almighty) is, but what he is not (quoted in Klauser 1981: 964), he nevertheless insists on associating the mind with the 'greatness of Christ'. He departs from the so-called negative proof of God, typical for mysticism; however—partly following the Platonic tradition—he ends up situating negativity in the service of positive reasoning.

It would be pointless to question the divine experiences of Plotinus or Clement. They have obviously obeyed the commands of their age when, in their desire for the absolute (and touched by the absolute), they only paid attention to fulfilment and, according to this, kept silent about the fragility of human existence. Thus, they successfully set themselves apart from the Gnostics too. In lieu of (also) taking inspiration from fragility, they protected themselves with the seemingly invulnerable shield of divine fulfilment. In a sense though, they fell into their own trap. Despite their insistence on the final non-existence of Unity, ultimately they played off moderation against excess, and certainty against the intangible.

This is why they lost their sense of balance. A condition of this is to refrain from only seeing deficiency and deprivation in excess but—in everyday parlance—also fulfilment. And conversely, in everything that appears obvious, unshakeable, we can sense a latent defect, the danger of deviation, the danger of blunder. At the beginning of our era, the Neoplatonians and then the Christians created the foundations of an overarching Church that rose above individuals. By contrast, the Gnostics offered lifestyle solutions to solitary individuals wishing to step out of communities. They wanted to break through the dome firmament in order to go up, unaided, to the heights. Their decisions were dictated by their fear of claustrophobia. The former put an emphasis on community and power; the latter were preoccupied with the dynamic of the soul and a withdrawal (or forward flight) from totality. One paid attention to the place, and the other to the fate of the individual. The former was a politician, the latter an existentialist; meanwhile, each recognized their own shadow in the Other. The belief in individual salvation (in possession of which it is possible to ignore community, society and even the entire world), the desire to break away from the world, the infinite trust placed in the 'soul' can only become imperative and widespread if the 'terror of history' becomes imminent (Sloterdijk 1993: 54). As soon as history as a construction emerges (the most convenient—and imperative—form of which is the story of Christian salvation), the partisans and pioneers of history show up on the scene, who flee forwards from closure and whose ultimate goal is actually located outside history. In Peter Sloterdijk's words: '[T]he Non-Existing, the Other, the Beyond, and the unknown passion for being distant from the world will take hold of these pioneers of history' (ibid.).

The Evil and the Disorderly

Above all, the Gnostics became aware of the anarchy inherent in existence and pointed out the incidental nature of everything.

Understandably, viewed from the perspective of community (the Church, *religio*), such a stance may appear destructive. Paul's Second Epistle to the Thessalonians is typical in this sense, in which he harshly critiques this very point of view. Let us pray, 'that we may be rescued from wicked and evil people', he urges his brethren (2 Thessalonians 3:2), and 'to keep away from believers who are living in idleness and not according to the tradition that they received from us' (3:6); finally: 'we hear that some of you are living in idleness, mere busybodies, not doing any work' (3:11). What Paul labels damaging, evil and morally questionable had initially meant in fact something extraordinary, remarkable, even wonderful (*atopos*: something that has no place). The evil (*ponéros*) in pre-Christian times was connected to trouble, to the burdensome and, consequently, to suffering and misery. The disorderly (*ataktos*) was initially a reference to something that did not observe order. Those who were preoccupied with futility (*periergazomai*) originally drew attention to the fact that they did not wish to achieve a tangible outcome at all costs. Socrates was a scholar of the earth and the sky, Plato notes in *The Apology of Socrates*, using the verb *periergazomai* (16b). For Paul, everything is morally questionable if the possibility of deviation from the designated route, of losing one's way, is inherent therein. In his usage, initially neutral expressions have become the building blocks for an expedient system. A precondition of system building is to refrain from such divine experiences that imply the possibility of vortexes, and where daze can undermine faith in order and intent. Paul is at a crossroads in world history: he throws ecstasy at the mercy of sober rhetoric (see Sloterdijk 1993: 123), and aims to persuade believers that there is a higher instance (community, Church, God) that can remove the burden of individual life from their shoulders. The Gnostics had been basically debating this very question all along and thus placed a burden on the individual's shoulders that has remained in place to this day. In sum, this difference could be formulated as follows: Paul's aim was to surrender divine experience to divine faith.

God's Name

Believers pray; however, what do those who are immersed in divine experience actually do? According to Gnostics, the world was created through the sevenfold laughter of the Ur-God (the unnameable, the non-existent); while the human being, forced to leave the maternal womb, was born crying. While crying, one acknowledges one's dues to laughter. Thus, the soul is crying and laughing at the same time. According to a theory of creation attributed to Abraxas, allegedly of magical powers, when God laughed for the seventh time, he took a deep breath and burst out crying while already laughing. This gave birth to the soul. This crying-laughing soul is the best representation of divine experience which is otherwise very difficult to put into words precisely due to the simultaneity of crying and laughing. In his Second Epistle to the Corinthians, Paul describes a vision in the course of which he 'was caught up into Paradise and heard things that are not to be told, that no mortal is permitted to repeat' (2 Corinthians 12:4). Instead of beginning to interpret these mysterious words, and following in their footsteps, he returns to the accessible. This, however, overshadows his faith in God: if in the throes of ecstasy, he experienced something that he is unable to talk about, then the seemingly accessible word 'God' sounds empty to him.

Gnostic sound-and-letter mysticism did its best to convey divine experience when it attempted to solve the meaning of the word 'God'. With their impossible, and at times comedic, attempts, they were trying after all to rescue divine experience from being captured and strangled by divine faith. Sound mysticism was naturally condemned to failure; nevertheless, it was well suited to reference such experiences that cannot be compartmentalized by the grammatical rules of language. This originated a development that cannot be restricted to the activity of Gnostics alone; the sound poetry of Hugo Ball or Kurt Schwitters indicate that such types of 'articulation' were in fact in demand in Christian cultural circles from the very beginning of Christianity. God's supposedly pronounceable name gave birth to a need for an unpronounceable language; what sounds like a nonsensical combination of sounds is in fact the shadow of the word 'God'. According to Marcion (second century), among the 'pronounceable' words we can form using the thirty letters, the possibility of the unpronounceable is imminently inherent, which means that the greater the empire of pronouncibility (the more words we can form), the greater that of the unpronounceable too. [The pronounceable Greek name of Jesus is made up of six sounds: Iota (4), Eta (3), Sigma (5), O (1), Epsilon (6), Sigma (5)—this, however, presupposes an unpronounceable 24-letter name.] His intricate attempt to trace existence back to the word beginning (*arkhé*) led him to a conclusion that could also perhaps come from Mallarmé, and could be the central idea of modern poetry: *intelligible words do not emerge from unpronounceability but themselves give birth to the unpronounceable.*

Whereof *one cannot speak*, thereof *one* must be *silent*: Wittgenstein's by-now-classic proposition creates the impression that this is a domain of the unpronounceable, somewhere beyond words, and it only depends on the ability, imagination and talent of the user whether they can penetrate this domain via the use of language. Divine faith relates to the concept of 'God', his name, on the basis of a similar idea. In the moments of divine experience, however, this idea loses its validity. In such cases, it emerges that the unpronounceable does not overtake the pronounceable but is, rather, in essence, identical with it. Words do not subjugate and restrict the unpronounceable but amplify it. In moments such as divine experience, when the individual breaks away from community and is all alone facing the incomprehensible, on the one hand, there are countless things to say, and, on the other, the mouth can barely utter anything. In order to describe this moment, one has to be a poet or give up on being understood. Language slips out of one's control. The name of the all-fertile Ur-mother is *Baatetophoth Zothakszathos*; the sceptre of Moira, in charge of the world, is called *Thoriobrititammaoraggadrioirdaggaroammatitirboiroth*; and according to Jeu's first book, if one utters the name of the all-penetrating force, then space ceases to exist and everything is laid bare (see *The Books of Jeu* 1978). This name is as follows: *aaa óóó zezórazazzzaieózaza eee iii zaieó-zóakhóe ooo üüü théézaozaez ééé zzeezaoza khózakhend tíikszaalethüks.*

According to the Gnostics, names have magical powers. In their view, when such a name is mentioned, God is also present by virtue of the act of naming. Signifier and signified become one and the same. The Gnostics believed that when uttering this name properly one had access to divine experience. It is not difficult to sense, however, that we are not talking about God's name in fact, but about an ecstatic shout. When shouting, one does not actually name God, but it is the God within us that shouts out. 'Look intently and make a long bellowing sound, like a horn, releasing all your breath and straining your sides' (*The 'Mithras' Liturgy* 1976). (Early Christian and pagan sects identified the presence of God in clicking, whistling, hissing, screaming, crying, rattling, even farting.)

The non-signifying sound that points beyond meaning does not communicate anything about God, because it is actually God himself that is being manifested in this sound—not as a person, not as a thing, but as a force. This sound could only be considered divine because at the very moment it was uttered, God himself had also made an appearance. This God is the God of divine experience, at the mercy of human mortality, and hence primarily tragic.

Moments of Devastating Sacredness

Inarticulacy, an area of particular focus for Gnosticism (or Jewish mysticism), stipulates that there are moments when one can have access to divine experience despite not even thinking of God. Divine faith usually connects to some religion or other; however, divine experience is also accessible if one does not accept any form of canonized religion whatsoever. The term 'divine experience' does not refer to a supposed God, but is a metaphoric label for a kind of dam burst, whereby something thereto alien and unimaginable penetrates into the world of order.

Inarticulate sounds tend to pour out of us when it is too late to compose ourselves. Such moments include pain, the loss of consciousness, sickness, gratification, the agony of death, vomiting. In each case there is a rupture of sorts; a fracture occurs in the well-oiled process of life. Most noticeable is the absence of transition. For this reason, we are tempted to interpret such moments as if there was a rupture in existence itself. Georges Bataille calls these moments sacred: in his view, in such situations we can hear God's voice, simultaneously approaching and yet fading away. For instance, when nausea takes hold of us, and the unique, unmistakeable smell of vomit—the smell of death—hits our nostrils, we feel as if we were on the threshold of annihilation. It is obvious that all this is happening to the self, and yet it feels as if the sole proof of one's being, one's very core were tumbling out. Human beings shaken in their sense of existence are watching while their bodies expel something—food for death; and if one were to glance at the face of a child staring paralysed at them, one would be able to see the reflection of death.

Inarticulate sounds, such as shouting and sighing, are of course not only manifestations of 'God' turned audible but also a form of echo. The invisible interior of the body resounds in this, something that pulsates at the core of all that is silence, and what could be called 'Ur-sound'. This is audible even in utmost silence. Heartbeat and pulsating veins are the sound of God inherent in humans. The more carefully one listens, the more frantic this sound gets, until it ruptures in the moments of grace and sacredness and floods everything. This situation is akin to the hermit in Wilhelm Heinrich Wackenroder's novella *A Wondrous Oriental Tale of a Naked Saint* who feels that he is tied to the wheels of time and hears its ceaseless rumble even when surrounded by complete silence:

Like a waterfall of thousands of roaring torrents which plunged down from the sky, eternally, eternally poured forth without a momentary pause, without a second's peace, thus it sounded in his ears and all his senses were intently focused solely on this. His labouring anguish became more and more caught up and carried away in the whirlpool of this wild confusion (1971: 175).

When noise breaks out of the human body, in moments of rattling or inarticulate groaning, what actually comes to the fore is something alien, yet it appears to be the raw material of life. God is 'not far from each one of us. For "In him we live and move and have our being"'—Paul contends on the Areopagus in relation to this 'raw material' (Acts of the Apostles 17:27–8). In the ecstatic moments of divine experience, this God leaves the 'upper regions' behind, moves into the human individual and designates the impossible as his centre. Meanwhile the latter, by ending up outside oneself (or, using an ecsystemic word, displaced), finds one's self in the unknown.

Annihilating Grace

Such experiences are usually called state of grace. Grace is a precondition of salvation according to Paul (Romans 5:2). Yet, if only this was at stake, then the state of grace would also allow for eternal life, and one would be absolved from the weight of mortality. According to this hypothesis, grace is a manifestation of positivity: it is fulfilment itself. However, it is the above-mentioned contradictory nature of fulfilment that actually interrogates the unanimity of grace. The Christian theory of grace is rooted in the belief that only God has access to the entirety of existence, only he has an overview of everything, which is why he is located beyond existence by definition. By handing over the keys of grace to God, this view acknowledges God as the absolute monarch—the guardian of totality. In the throes of divine experience, one is able to witness the possibility of withdrawal from existence and thus starts a rebellion against God and totality. This feels as if one had to first demolish one's own prison walls in order to be able to breathe freely. For this reason, in Greek mythology, grace and revenge could appear as manifestations of one and the same Goddess; the Charis communicated in equal measure with the sky and the deep seas, not to mention the Underworld. According to the Greeks, the three Charis were not only daughters of Zeus and Eurynome, but also of Nuxe, the night, and Erebos, the lightless obscurity of the depths. If we were to accept this pedigree, then the Charis are also granddaughters of Chaos. They are messengers of charm and joy, yet also of Persephone, whom they accompany on her passage from the Underworld to day-light. On occasion, Aphrodite is also called Charis, which is to remind us that she is not only the Goddess of love but also of debauched sexuality and, at times, of war. The one-word Greek term 'Charis' could only be translated into Latin using two words: Venus (beauty and love) and Gratia (grace, thankfulness); not to mention that Christians went as far as to remove the word's earthly (and underworldly) connotations, so that it eventually emerged as *gratia*, beyond any inner conflict and devoid of all flesh and blood.

In the course of divine experience, grace manifests its Greek and dualistic qualities. This sense of grace does not promise a return to totality but unites the extremes without reconciling them with one another. One becomes aware of the actual absence of God while, in fact, finding God; and it is in such moments of grace that one gains a so-called experience of completeness. These moments, however, also make one experience the fact that completeness can-not be imagined without its shadow, which—in the absence of a better word—they named Nothingness.

The Death of God

This is the reason why grace can become a messenger of annihila-tion: not only of people but of existence itself. This lends meaning to the cross of Jesus, 'by which the world has been crucified to me, and I to the world' (Galatians 6:14). This cross holds together the various facets of existence, in a manner described by Plato in *Timaeus* (36b); and its function is to ensure that everything connects with everything else. According to the apocryphal Acts of Andrew, the cross holds the entire cosmos in its embrace: its top reaches the heavens and points to Logos; its left and right sides keep chaos at bay and hold the cosmos together; its bottom stretches down to the lower depths, so it can connect the below to the above. In moments of grace and divine experience, Man is 'crucified' upon such a cross, thus realizing that existence is marked by its very absence, order is made up of chaos, and what is high above (God) can mean eternal death just as well as the one that lies below (Hell) can mean eternal life. Finding oneself at the very centre of the cross, the individual is tempted by conversations about God, despite experiencing annihilation. 'My God, my God, why have you forsaken me?' Jesus cried out at the moment of his death (Matthew 27:46). The darkness that then enshrouded the earth heralded the death of God; and the subsequent earthquake and rocks cracking open marked crucifixion as an irrevocable event. This instance, however, was not just the moment of death for Jesus but for God too. God sent Jesus to earth so that he (God) would not have to exercise judgement over people from afar but, through Jesus, would be able to undergo every possible human experience from within (see Balthasar 1969: 215). However, since he sent Jesus to Earth, he had no choice but to expose him sooner or later to death too. If God really wanted to exercise judgement over people from within, he had to also share their state of dispossession and self-emptying (*kenosis*). He needed to get to know both the experience of God's denial and that of being forsaken by God. Upon Christ's death, God did not forsake Jesus but, in and through Jesus, experienced death. In order to be able to resurrect in the human being, God had to experience being forsaken by God, in other words, experience his own death. God moves into the individual at the very moment of crucifixion, with the express aim to die that same instant.

The cross is a symbol of devastating sacredness, annihilating grace and divine experience. This mentality based on aims and directions that carefully differentiates between fulfilment and dis-possession does not fracture in the moment of grace. Thus it becomes apparent that God, whom one saw as the custodian of pragmatism and conformity, is nascent in inexpediency, and in the extreme and paradoxical moments of grace. The God whom believers consider to be fulfilment is but a mere nomer, which makes an attempt at concealing this other God that is actually being born, which is only nascent with a view to die. This other God con-fronts the human being with its own fragility. This 'new' God is not a person, not an independently existing (or not-existing) being but a vortex emerging in the soul. Immersed in this phenomenon, one finds oneself while being lost for the world—having the sensation of being crucified as well as being aware that one's own self is not so obvious as previously expected. Thus, one experiences a 'subjec-tive galaxy' (Sloterdijk 1993: 17), of which one is creator and suf-ferer alike.

CHAPTER 2

WHO LIGHTENS?
(WHO FLASHES WITH LIGHTNING?)

Joseph Beuys, *Lightning with Stag in Its Glare*

Lava looks like clotted blood. Dried-out lumps protrude from it, as if they were relics of the wounds of the earth. The earth is gravity above all; and yet, when volcanoes erupt, the earth is on an upward flight: trying to free itself from its own self. A new creation is about to begin. Fires light up from below, the nether darkness is trying to transcend itself in the guise of an underground torrent of lightning. The dried-out, heavy and solid bits of lava are imprints of the fire raging down below. The earth did not succeed in leaving its course after all, and, in this sense, lava is also an embodiment of failure.

Lava stone is a monument of the earth besides itself; a tangible manifestation of excess. Its lame immovability stands for the suppression of an unimaginable struggle. The impossible is embodied in it; something beyond description or perception, something that does not allow anything to identify with itself. Akin to the crater, a visible facet of universal chaos, this eyeball of the earth reminiscent of the wound, lava stone is a messenger of an all-subversive struggle. Existence made an attempt at rupture in the midst of a lightning torrent of fire, and the impossible emerged under the guise of rough, solid rock.

The fire of the gods drives us to set forth by day
And by night. So come, let us look at what is apparent.

Friedrich Hölderlin (2004: 9)

The divine fire mentioned by Hölderlin emanates light, day and night in equal measure. It dissipates the darkness of the night and exceeds the light of the day. What sort of light might it have? Can this light be perceived at all? *The Cross in the Forest*, a painting by Caspar David Friedrich, a contemporary of Hölderlin, might offer a good illustration. It depicts two sources of light: one is 'natural', the other 'artificial', radiating from the cross in the background. The latter is virtual light, and is perhaps not even visible to everyone except for the deserving. And it is possible that what they are seeing is not the light itself. If this light is beyond clarity and obscurity, beyond day and night, then it is also invisible. Divine fire does not illuminate but, according to Hölderlin, reveals; and it makes Man, routinely leading their lives according to the cycle of day and night, reveal themselves. The flame of divine fire makes the world reveal itself, and by the same token, when touched by fire, Man also opens up.

In this state of being laid bare, however, Man becomes defence-less and vulnerable, and, in Hölderlin's words, gets carried away by a 'jubilant madness'. Hölderlin also evokes the god of ecstasy, the torn-apart and tortured Dionysus. He is the god of the past, who nevertheless points to the future ('the gods enter'). Mentioning Dionysus, however, Hölderlin does not only allude to Crucifixion and Resurrection (in this way referencing Christ without naming him) but also to excessive madness (which is hard to reconcile with the Christian idea of Christ). Heraclitus noted in relation to mad-ness: 'For if it were not to Dionysus that they made the procession and sung the hymn to the shameful parts, the deed would be most shameless; but Hades and Dionysus, for whom they rave and celebrate Lenaean rites, are the same' (in Kirk and Raven 1957: fr. 247).

Divine fire lays the human being bare, who, as a result, discovers the common denominator between light and dark, as well as life and death. This is experienced as a mysterious flame, the light of which ruptures the darkness of the night and the light of the day.

The Ecstasy of Semele

Let us continue to dwell on Dionysus, whose birth was the result of none other than mysterious fire. His birth was facilitated by a 'brand of heaven's hot splendour' (Euripides, *The Bacchae* 3) and his father was Zeus himself. To be precise, it was lightning, into which Zeus transformed himself when he visited the mortal daughter of Kadmos, Semele. She wanted, at least once, to cast her eyes on her mysterious lover with whom she could only meet under cover of the night. Apollodorus sums up their story as follows:

> But Zeus loved Semele and bedded with her unknown to Hera. Now Zeus had agreed to do for her whatever she asked, and deceived by Hera she asked that he would come to her as he came when he was wooing Hera. Unable to refuse, Zeus came to her bridal chamber in a chariot, with lightnings and thunderings, and launched a thunderbolt. But Semele expired of fright, and Zeus, snatching the six-month abortive child from the fire, sewed it in his thigh (Apollodorus, *The Library* 2.4.3).

Lightning struck the earthly princess to death, while her son by Zeus was being born 'in the white heart of the fire' (Euripides, *The Bacchae* 115), and deadly fire turned out to be life-giving.

Prior to this, Semele had never seen Zeus in his celestial manifestation. Her future fate had appeared to her once in a dream but this was a mild vision: she pictured herself as a tree, the roots of which were watered by the eternal dew of Kronos' son (see Harrison 1962: 173). Her fate turned out to be crueller though. Following her death, she ended up in the underworld, from where she was brought back to earth by her son. 'Thus men perceived that he was a god and honoured him; and having brought up his mother from Hades and named her Thyone, he ascended up with her to heaven' (Apollodorus, *The Library* 3.5.3). The meaning of her new name is Adoringly Frantic. Semele became immortal due to her adoration and frenzy. Her new name hints at the state of ecstasy that overwhelmed her in her wedding chamber following the lightning strike.

According to Pausanias (*Description of Greece* 9.12.3), it was forbidden for anyone to enter this room on the Acropolis of Thebes. For mortals, it must have been particularly confusing to negotiate a simultaneous death and birth. Understandably, several people tried to 'tame' this story: 'My mother sinned, said they; and in her need, / With Cadmus plotting, cloaked her human shame / With the dread name of Zeus; for that the flame / From heaven consumed her, seeing she lied to God' (Euripides, *The Bacchae* 35–8). This explanation is dubiously rational; it sidelines precisely what it should explain: the miracle of the all-subverting moment, as if one tried to channel the flashes of passion using an 'enlightened' lightning rod.[1]

---

1 With reference to lightning, Hermann Andreas Pistorius, in 1785, attempted to call attention to the power of enlightened thought: 'While those revering thunder and lightning tried to avoid the damaging effects of lightning by means of prayer and sacrifice, philosophers found refuge from the fear and superstition caused by storms in reason, observed the similarity between lightning and electricity and finally discovered the beneficent lightning rod' (Pistorius 1785: 256, quoted in Raulff 1988: p. 75). Hermann Melville's short story 'The Lightning-Rod Man', however, focuses on a protagonist who chases away the lightning-rod salesman: 'you mere man who come here to put you and your pipestem between clay and sky, do you think that because you can strike a bit of green light from the Leyden jar, that you can thoroughly avert the supernal bolt? Your rod rusts, or breaks, and where are you? Who has empowered you, you Tetzel, to peddle round your indulgences from divine

A whole lot more is at stake here: the secret of the lightning of the god of gods; the unravelling of Hölderlin's 'divine fire' which makes one open-minded and fragile at once, and as a consequence of which one partakes of an event that could be called 'divine experience'.

Secret Ordainment

The light of lightning presents the world from a new vantage point and brands it as ephemeral. This sight cannot be easily reconciled with regular notions of time and space. Hölderlin writes in relation to the Eternal Father that 'Under a thundering sky / His sign is silent' (2007: 45). Although lightning is accompanied by thunder, rumbling and raging wind, and nature appears to become unhinged, everything is muted for a moment as if it were to resettle for good and the world froze into an ultimate tableau. In daylight or at night, everything lives its own life: 'all things are steered through all,' contends Heraclitus (Kirk and Raven 1957: fr. 230). In the actual moment when lightning occurs, however, this randomness appears fatefully rearranged and organized, and everything points at a secret purpose and designation. 'And silence took the air, and no leaf stirred / In all the forest dell' while, prior to the laceration of Pentheus, Dionysus' bright holy fire, lightning 'came / Twixt earth and sky a pillar of high flame' (Euripides, *The Bacchae* 1331–3). Lightning holds everything together, it enshrouds the world in a sinister light and establishes mysterious connections. According to Heraclitus, 'Thunderbolt steers all things' (Kirk and Raven 1957: fr. 223). The power of lightning is really mysterious. It originates in Nothingness and turns into Nothing, but while it lasts it outrivals everything. Everything is subordinated to it; and by comparison, everything becomes void.

---

ordinations? The hairs of our heads are numbered, and the days of our lives. In thunder as in sunshine, I stand at ease in the hands of my God. False negotiator, away!' (Melville 1984: 762)

The Moment of Combustion

Catching a glimpse of Zeus and being struck by lightning, Semele must have appeared like a landscape enshrouded in the light of lightning. Adoringly Frantic: overpowered and enthralling at the same time. In her role as a victim of excess, she ended up at the mercy of immortality. As if, through her, the moment of combustion had expanded into the infinite.

We have a lot of information about Semele's life prior to and following the lightning. Yet hearing her name we tend to conjure up the same image, immortalized by the sixteenth-century French artist Antoine Caron. This is the moment of her combustion, of her immortality and glorification. Confined to fire, she is all alone and beaming. This moment is unique and everlasting. Semele's eternity is not rooted in endless time but in an intensity that cannot be heightened any further. It was this that set fire to her bridal bed; and, under the guise of lightning, made herself unbearable to her own self.

The Lightning Flashes of Creation

People tend to get reverential when gazing at the lightning sky. As if they were experiencing some sort of an initiation, taking place not only in ancient times but even now, in the twenty-first century. Jakob Böhme claims that 'life is engendered' by lightning (2010: 3.25), and his hypothesis rings back to ancestral notions. Most mythologies connect the first gods to lightning.[2] In all cases, lightning is situated

---

2 The Babylonian Adad, son of the chief god, held a sheaf of lightning in his hand and both heaven and earth would give way to him; lightning was the symbol of Al-maqah, protector god of the kingdom of Saba; Baal-Hadad, ancient god of Syria, would be accompanied by lightning at all times; Q'uq'umatz, 'the heart of heavens', the god of K'iche' indigenous Americans, created the earth, the plants and the animals by way of lightning; the all-engendering and life-giving Tirawa, the god of the indigenous American Pawnee people, got an insight into existence disguised as lightning; Yima, the

in relation to the creation of existence. Lightning ruptures the sky and blinding light floods through these root-shaped cracks. According to several mythologies, the dark water-like maternal womb of existence was impregnated by a god who by definition was male and aided by lightning. In this instance, lightning is a phallus that spills its seed into the water, following which it loses its strength. Lightning was also the cosmic sexual organ of the Vedic fire god Agni, known as the 'bull dwelling in water'; and his wife Kali was thought to have 'put out a flaming lingam in her yoni' (see Walker 1983: 539). (The meaning of the name of the Indian city of Darjeeling is: *dorje* + *lingam* = lightning phallus [Harrison 1962: 77].) The lotus flower, the tantric symbol of masculinity, was denoted with the word *vajra*, which meant both phallus, i.e. beaming lightning (this word is etymologically related to the Germanic 'awakening' = enlightening), and diamond (Eliade 1958: 253).[3] Christianity incorporated traces of this idea: the baptismal font has often been likened to Mary's womb (Mary was thought to have been impregnated by holy fire, *igne sacro inflammata*), and during the consecration of churches, burning candles would often be extinguished in the water therein (Neumann 1955: 311–12).

Thus, when visiting Semele disguised as lightning, Zeus involved her into the very act of creation. Like the majority of storm gods, Zeus–Jupiter also put in occasional appearances while riding the bull, the symbol of fertility, holding a phallic sceptre in his hand, which he later swapped for a double-bitted axe, the labrys, with

---

ancient god of Iranian mythology, was given birth in the shape of lightning in a pillar of fire—he was born in a golden age when death was yet unknown; lightning symbolizes Ngai, the chief god of the East African Bantu; the Khmer Preas Eyn, correspondent of the chief Vedic god Indra, steps out with a sheaf of lightning in his hand. One could continue this lineage further, with the Etruscan Aplu and Summamus, Deng from Sudan, the Inca Illapa, Pele from Hawaii, the old Illyrian Perendi.

3 In the Brihadaranyaka Upanishad, the husband says to his wife: 'I am the heavens, and you are the earth' (quoted in Eliade 1958: 254).

which he would throw thunderbolts at his enemies. Consequently, lightning is not only weapon but also *phallos*. (The sixteenth-century etching by Master L. D., to be found in the Albertina Museum in Vienna, depicts Semele receiving the thunderbolts in an unmistakeably orgasmic state—as if enslaved by the Buddhist goddess Pandara whose two defining elements are fire and passionate love.) If we take into account the additional fact that Semele is not only mortal but also an *earthly being*, considered to be the Goddess of the Earth by the Thracians and known as Gaia, then through their encounter and embrace we are in fact dealing with a creation myth proper.

The ancient Greeks linked the union of body and soul to lightning, the weapon of Zeus (it is lightning that bestows the soul upon a nascent body). At the same time, lightning is also the guardian of death: it not only gives life but also imparts death. Zeus struck Asclepius dead with a thunderbolt, angered by the latter's temerity to resurrect the dead; and then Apollo killed the Cyclopes in an act of revenge, for it was them who had forged this deadly weapon for Zeus in the first place. In the greatest battle of all times, the Battle of the Titans, it was lightning again that turned out to be the most fatal weapon: 'From Heaven and Olympus (Zeus) came forthwith, hurling his lightning: the bold flew thick and fast from his strong hand together with thunder and lightning, whirling an awesome flame. The life-giving earth crashed around in burning, and the vast wood crackled loud with fire all about' (Hesiod, *Theogony* 689–94).

Hesiod gives this account of the decisive battle, adding mysteriously: 'Astounding heat seized Chaos' (ibid.: 799). The fate of the Titans does not end here, though. According to orphic cosmogony, the first man emerged from the ashes and cinder left behind from the Titans struck by lightning, and thus their birth, like that of Dionysus (whom, as it happens, the Titans had torn apart and devoured), is rooted in devastation occasioned by lightning. This explains why certain mysteries, in which the initiated would not only prepare for death itself but also for a confrontation with its devastating impact, would summon up lightning and thunder, and why Pythagoras arriving at Crete was purified with the help of an aerolite ('meteoric thunderstone') that had, according to hypotheses circulating at the time, made it to earth by way of lightning (Porphyry, *The Life of Pythagoras* 17).

According to some mythologies, lightning is the apple of God's eye: in the course of lighting, God has an insight into earthly life. Looking at the light of lightning, one can rightly feel that one's glance is braided with that of God. This is the origin of reverential gaze. And if 'God' looks down through the cracks of heaven, the light of lightning freezes the world into a photographic tableau and, for an instant, reveals the thing that holds everything together and ensures that all there is should continue to exist. It is this shared fate, this *there-is* that protrudes through the cracks of heaven. This is why everything that so far appeared a random mass, suddenly looks preordained. The inconceivable takes shape in lightning; and owing to the fact that things conceal it, what in normal circumstances remains unseen now becomes visible. Mythology situates lightning at par with God— despite the fact that in the moment of lightning, it becomes apparent that the term 'God' is but a distorted echo of something that can never be foregone.

The Hearth

Pausanias tells us that in the Arcadian Lykaion, there was a holy site of Zeus that was out of bounds for all: the Lykaios. If entering this site despite the warning, human or animal would not be able to cast a shadow, because light originates here (*Description of Greece* 8.38.6). In Lykaios, home of thundering Zeus, the all-destroying light of lightning is incessant and must have been akin to the seat of Heraclitus' everlasting fire, whom the Pythagorean Philolaos called Hestia, the hearth of the universe, the house of Zeus, the mother of God, and the altar, encounter and measure of nature

(Diels–Kranz 44A16; see Diels 1952, hereafter DK). Whoever settles at this hearth can rightly sense that they have arrived at the source of existence. The absence of shadow is a fabulous symbol for an absolute identification with oneself. Nothing could shed light on the individual, because the latter is a source of light in itself. In order for this to happen, however, one has to say farewell to the world of shadows.

Far from the world and close to the fire: this is the moment of divine experience. The state of being at the mercy of the world ends here, and this occurs without losing one's sense of self. On the contrary—it marks the beginning of finding oneself.

The Silver Flash

Lightning first united the two lovers, and then separated them from each other. Semele combusted in the flames, and this wounded Zeus, too, by depriving him of his love. According to mythology, it was Zeus who brought the lightning bolts; but since lightning is not only a divine 'weapon' but also a source of energy that has impact everywhere, it is possible that lightning also struck out of Semele's eyes. She was not only struck dead by lightning but, in the moment of combustion, she also started to flash with lightning herself. Her gaze must have been just as burning as that of Zeus.

Franz von Baader calls this 'the silver flash' (*Silberblick* in German, also meaning squint-eyed), which allows for simultaneous vision with both the inner and outer eye (1851–60: VOL. 7, 142). Lovers discover each other with such a silver flash when setting eyes on each other for the first time, compared with which all subsequent glances are increasingly blurry. The gaze is 'the most burning' in the moment of love (in German, the terms for 'lightning' and 'glance', as well as 'moment' stem from the same root): in such situations, one rightly feels that the face has a secret mission, compared with which the configuration of previous features was a mere rehearsal. The passionless gaze relates to enamoured glance in the same way as a passport photo to the real face. And since passport photos represent people as if they were criminals, looking back from the state of passion, lovers feel that their previous lives were spent in sin: the sin of neglecting the dramatic flash of fulfilment.

Aided by the silver flash, the eye does not 'feel up' the face of the other and does not assemble it from bits and pieces; rather, the face lights up like a spark. It is fitting to say that those in love discover their own self in the other: all the pressure points of their being are instantly channelled in the same direction, only to meet in a single face. It is impossible to assess whether those in love recognize themselves in their beloved because they have come across that initial unity again, the absence of which has made them lead their lives in a state of continuous longing; or that this unity is being achieved for the first time now, and is hence also a union, until the fulfilment of which those falling in love for the first time could have had no inkling that their previous life was a mere fraction of the whole. In any case, we are dealing with a fracture through which the unknown penetrates into life—a crack reminiscent of the cracks in the sky.

The recognition of unity, of lovers finding each other in the wake of the silver flash, is also a sign of crisis. According to Baader, aided by the silver flash, lovers also discover the eternal, the image of the nascent god, in the face of the other (ibid.: VOL. 4, 99). Failing that, they would not be able to recognize themselves in the face of the other; and we would be left to our own devices for good were we not made in the image of God. Lovers are so intent on clinging to each other's face because they instinctively feel that they are at the mercy of an unknown force that subjugates them. This force is known in the European tradition as 'God'. It is common knowledge that the more elemental the passion, the least tangible the other party. Yet this 'Other' is not intangible, seeing that they willingly allow themselves to be wrestled with and devoured: after all, they would like to give themselves 'wholly' to their lover. It is the God within that is hard to approach, and it is this God that alienates those at whom love is directed; this unknown force ensures that lovers feel dazzled and realize they have lost themselves. 'God is nearer to me than I am to myself' (Eckhart 1909: 19); and, having found their supposed centre, Man starts to experience the impossible. The unquenchable longing that gives rise to love reveals that the individual is unable to transcend itself. The more elemental the love, the more excruciating the sensation of this vulnerability; and there comes a point beyond which lovers get burnt by this very sense of the impossible.

For this reason, the moment of love is not only about finding oneself but also about dispossession. While those in love are able to compress into someone else all the desire and longing that they have previously considered to be their own, and could not handle to a satisfactory extent, they also find that they ended up beyond themselves. They found their centre, yet this happens to be located outside the boundary of their selves. This does not mean that the existing centre has suddenly 'shifted' into another being, but, rather, that this centre has just come into being—*sameness is the outcome of difference*. In parallel with the 'lightning flash' and the 'silver flash', it becomes increasingly likely that the individual should lose itself at the very point when it supposedly found itself, because existence itself lacks a centre. Its alleged 'basis' is Being, which permeates everything yet remains on the outside, so it becomes noticeable only in the void inherent in things. Whenever one tries to 'pull oneself together', one cannot help finding oneself set into motion by a faith placed in some sort of a supposed centre. Beyond a certain point, however, it becomes obvious that this is impossible. The more existence 'thickens', the less one can find one's way around, and ultimately all one is in a position to perceive is the fact of being at the mercy of the impossible.

Beyond Divine Kindness and Diabolical Evil

In the course of the silver flash, the gaze is instantaneous like lightning; under the influence of Hölderlin's 'divine fire', it is accompanied by an enlightenment, a revelation that transcends both light and dark. The soul 'sparkles', the explanation for which, in the European metaphysical tradition, is generally God's gesture of grace. Historically distant texts, such as the Chaldean prophecies, would have named the 'part' of the soul related to God a 'spark', based on the association that lightning was the device with which the Father 'intervened' in the world (see Nilsson 1961: VOL. 2, 480). This sentence harks back to Plato's 'Seventh Letter' in which he claimed:

> But thus much I can certainly declare concerning all these writers, or prospective writers, who claim to know the subjects which I seriously study [...]. It is impossible, in my judgement at least, that these men should understand anything about this subject [...]. For it does not at all admit of verbal expression like other studies, but, as a result of continued application to the subject itself and communion therewith, it is brought to birth in the soul on a sudden, as light that is kindled by a leaping spark, and thereafter it nourishes itself (*Epistles* 341c–d).

Mechtild of Magdeburg noted in the thirteenth century: 'When God sees fit to let his divine heart shine forth in love toward the very blessed soul so intensely that a small spark alights on the cold soul and [...] the heart of this person begins to glow' (1998: 238). Jakob Böhme calls human life itself a spark, which has sprung from divine grace: 'For what is the life of the creature? Nothing else but a spark (quoting Meister Eckhart's term, *vünkelin*) of the will of God' (2010: 66.64). In fact, Böhme attributes the capacity for sight to this very spark. In this view, it is not looking as such but the 'glimpse of the eye of the mind' that 'goeth through wood and stone, through bones and marrow, and there is nothing that can withhold it, for it pierceth and breaketh the darkness everywhere without rending the body of any thing' (1910: 16.6).

Without fail, all these explanations connect the state of being enlightened to divine kindness. The nature of sparks and lightning examined to date reminds us, however, that the act of lighting a spark, in other words, lightning, does not only engender new life but also causes destruction. It does not only offer the prospect of being more discerning but also makes us blind. No wonder, therefore, that in parallel with defying the idea of divine kindness, the 'advocates' of evil have put forward their own self-made and equally one-track notions. According to the Egyptians, the father of lightning was Seth, an immortal snake (Satan in Hebrew); and although at a later stage Matthew gives voice to his conviction that 'For as the lightning comes from the east and flashes as far as the west, so will be the coming of the Son of Man' (Matthew 24:27), Jesus dissociates himself from lightning and says to his disciples: 'I watched Satan fall from heaven like a flash of lightning' (Luke 10:18). In lieu of the son of man, it is Evil that charges through the sky disguised as lightning. Evil radiates and carries light, which is why Lucifer (Satan's Latin name is Lucifer = carrier of light) was symbolized in the East with a trifurcate *phallos*-lightning (with which—according to later fathers of the Church—he would aim at church steeples).[4]

Concepts that exclusively associate lightning with decay and eternal death are just as one-sided as those that connect it to divine kindness. Both options examine the phenomenon of intensity that ruptures life like lightning, solely from the point of view of its

---

4 Franz von Baader observed this dual aspect of lightning: 'Lightning is also a gatekeeper, a door opener, and to this end all senses are concentrated in the lighting bolt.—It simultaneously opens and closes, in other words, when it comes to those inclined towards goodness (those who lend themselves to cosmic assimilation), it facilitates access to higher regions, and when it comes to rebels it condemns them, like an ostracizing judge, to the darkness below.— To this end, this fiery bolt releases its world of light from itself and encompasses the world of darkness therein (and below itself)' (1851–60: VOL. 2, 30).

consequences; yet, owing to its very intensity, this precedes time—in other words, the possibility of separating cause and effect. In such intensely lightning moments, it is the impossible that cripples Man, akin to Paul as painted by Caravaggio in *The Conversion of Saint Paul*. In this painting, Paul is not exposed to divine kindness, nor is he the victim of evil, but of excess. In Baader's terms: lightning is the act of a bottomless abyss, of the absence of foundation (*Ungrund*), which cancels out all actual foundations (*Grund*) (1851–60: VOL. 2, 239–40).[5] He who sends the flashes of lightning perturbs and dehumanizes those whom he targets. Such moments cannot form the basis for any future whatsoever; consequently, divine kindness ends up being just as meaningless as diabolical evil.

The Ground Zero of Existence

When lightning strikes, time is compressed into a single intense moment. Touched by this moment, the gaze also emits flashes; radiating a sense of pure alienation. It becomes obvious in such moments that the centreless-ness of existence is not something that has an impact somewhere afar but, rather, within us. We are in fact the very embodiment of centreless-ness: at the height of the moment, everything is channelled towards this single centre, which then disintegrates as we are attempting to grab it. It remains the object of eternal longing.

When talking about Nothingness, one tries, almost involuntarily, to convey intangibility—the intangibility of existence. Conjuring up Nothingness, one denies everything that exists, yet, however—

5 The most defining moment of Martin Luther's life was also connected to lightning. On 2 July 1505, at about 6 kilometres from Erfurt, he got caught up in a storm. Lightning struck in his immediate vicinity and wounded his leg. Scared to death, he burst out: 'Saint Anne, please help me, and I shall become a monk!' Following this, he did indeed join holy orders, and kept mentioning throughout his life that an otherworldly force from had interfered with his life at that time. His father suspected the temptation of the devil, but Luther himself saw this as a sign of divine vocation (see Brecht 1981: 57).

as a consequence of terminology—also posits something: something that does not exist (since it is Nothingness), but which has an existence of sorts (since it has experiential qualities). In relation to 'Nothingness', the paradoxical situation arises whereby Being penetrates everything and is equally 'close' to everything there is; at the same time, it is inaccessible because it backs out of everything.

For this reason, moments with absolute validity and devoid of a sense of direction or goal, past or future, have a lightning effect: they shed light on the carefully concealed facet of human life whereby, behind the scenes, one does not consist of directions, goals, plans, causes and effects, but is, rather, the ground zero of existence (and not the omega-point theorized by Franz von Baader and Teilhard de Chardin, which is the culmination of a pragmatic and meaningful cosmological process), and the most specific facets of one's nature are excluded from events. Everything starts and also ends with this; and despite arguments to the contrary, no one can take away the certainty that death marks the end of everything and that being at the mercy of existence is absolute.

Of course, the individual does its best to encounter such a hypothetical centre: it surrounds itself with the illusion of reason and goal, tries to find refuge in communities, and relies on religion or science for comfort. In other words, one uses the methods of domestication, and European culture has always been of considerable assistance to this end. Our culture, having developed increasingly sophisticated notions of progress—labelled as either Christian, evolutionist or 'objectively scientific'—has always handled the magic of now with reservation. The early Church fathers would have started cursing whenever the subject of mysteries came up; when it came to the Gnostics, they would revert to endless sophistry. In the Middle Ages, sceptics were literally driven mad, magicians were denounced as charlatans, fanatics were excommunicated and mystics were treated with utter reservation. When, by the end of the eighteenth century, God had reached a level of depersonalization and—in William Blake's words—started to look like an oil lamp that ran out of fuel, those who trusted their inner experiences above the teachings of science were labelled mad; were considered fanatics who had spent too much time on futile things; were seen as having an aesthetic disposition (*bel esprits*) and forced to retreat; were deemed irrational and felt ill at ease in hierarchical situations; were labelled nihilists who did not want to cooperate; and were declared terrorists who would want to compress life into a single all-encompassing moment. But since all-combusting moments, in which the omnipotent force of culture and history loses its certainty, tend to periodically come to the fore, the culture of modernity has adopted the tempting method of domestication: it has declared the arts a sort of reservation in which one can yield to the enjoyment of the here and now with impunity. Yet 'the most liberating effect of art is that it makes one doubt whether one does exist' (Unamuno 2000: 289). This idea was not formulated by an artist for no reason: only artists can state such a thing with impunity—in the event that even they actually can—without the guardians of culture attempting to whip-steer the arts into the cattle pen of pragmatism. This should not take us by surprise since we are dealing with a culture oriented towards the future—and hence subject to the rules of time, and underpinned by a complex network of institutions. The intensity of the here and now lays the world bare, exposes the aimlessness and slipperiness of everything, generates schisms in belief and, most importantly, exposes us to the mercy of the incommunicable and the indefinable. The hear and now is subversive and anarchic, and opens up a pathway towards the contemplation of death. It offers extraordinary insight (enlightenment), yet this is only so in-depth because it cannot be arranged according to an organized system. It cannot be forged into ideology, since it resists all attempts at institutionalization.

The Face

Let us return to the look inflamed with passion and the burning silver flash. When lightning strikes, it seems as if the features of a face appears on the sky. The root-like cracks remind us of Nothing and No one; they are whimsical and impossible to replicate. This whim, this excessive tyranny, transcends everything to such an extent that in the moment of lightning, everything becomes insignificant, and the unpredictable comes into unquestionable force.

But does this characterize all faces? Is it not what is in fact impossible to replicate, the 'never again' that becomes exclusive in each and every face? Lightning reminds us of an unearthly face; but strangely enough, the human face is the most eye-catching when, following a mysterious force, everything is compressed in the gaze, and the tension, instead of decreasing as usual prior to dying out, is being discharged in the shape of lightning. On such occasions, the face flashes; it becomes not only fragmented like the sky but also all-oppressive. The unpredictable, so far latent and carefully disguised, emanates from it. The lightning gaze is 'inhuman', yet it is also most human: it is distorted into the unreliable when one is confronted with one's genuine, thereto unacknowledged situation. In conditions of peace and quiet, there is no lightning; one is fully at ease, unreservedly embracing being at one with its selfhood. Such a face is comforting. The gaze starts flashing with lightning when this sameness unravels and one is being charged with a matter that is perceived as alien. Is it not odd that a face becomes arresting, genuinely human, at the very moment of being permeated by strangeness? Could it be that one actually finds oneself in the very act that actually lays one bare? A face is the more irresistible, the more difficult it is to approach and address it. In such situations, even the most reliable and familiar faces can become estranged. As if faces would turn their backs to the human world, and the gaze would intertwine with the unfamiliarity that is beyond everything human.

Such a gaze tries in vain to entice the Other; the lightning of the unknown, the non-human, the Other cannot be grounded with any lightning rod whatsoever. It is the impossible that is burning in such a gaze, the same impossible that is embodied in the lightning that cracks the sky open.

It is remarkable that the features of all faces are ordered in the same way, and as a result, they have started to look like one another. This similarity is just as eerie as the landscape enshrouded in lightning; and in such situations, an irresistible and alarming truth starts to emerge. No two faces are alike; and yet there are moments when the similarities are more striking than the differences.

It becomes apparent that faces are neither a biological and anthropological given, nor the imprints of a unique, peerless arrangement of life. The former is typical for animals, in whose gaze one can identify the traces of individuality, but these are not distinct enough to eclipse the dominance of similarity. By contrast, human beings are exceptional: like all animals, humans are unique yet they also have an insight into their individuality. They are beings tuned in to their own existence, who are aware of their situation. The unmistakable quality of their facial features mirrors this, reflecting their coming to terms with uniqueness. The uniqueness of the human face indicates that one does not only live but also experiences life. From the arrangement of facial features, one can also decipher the exact way in which human beings lead and organize their lives from birth to death. By virtue of their face, humans supersede not only rocks and plants but also animals. And yet, it is common occurrence that faces turn beastly, that their beauty is reminiscent of the aimless existence of plants, and that their inexpressiveness starts to resemble that of rocks. As if an unknown force, undermining insight and consciousness, can oppress the human being and throw it outside itself. In fear of an absent centre, one tries to rely on a higher-ranking God, and, similarly, seeks to find answers to the periodical and mysterious alteration of facial features. One strives to discover the most straightforward manifestation of the image of God in the human face, which—according to the interpretation of Saint Bonaventura—has its inferior and superior versions, depending on whether the soul has to do with the world of creatures or the divine Trinity.

Yet, this explanation loses its validity in the scorching moment of the lightning gaze. The most varied faces are arranged in similar ways; but it is not the lightning of God but of the impossible that ploughs over and dehumanizes them. Should we insist on God's name, we need to imagine a paralysing and alienating God that deters one even from one's own self. If the gaze starts flashing with lightning, faces emanate alienation and this makes them mask-like and prone to resembling one another. One does not only look *at* the world using its face and gaze, but also looks *through* it. One is in pursuit of the unknown; but since this is latent in everything, it also permeates the gaze: and it is the unknown that is inherent in the gaze looking for the unknown. This is not only about the fact that one is surrounded by something that it tries to make sense of yet sooner or later will get stuck, irrespective of their abilities, intuition, intelligence or resourcefulness. This explains the unique arrangement of faces only to a degree. The unknown, the ungraspable is not merely an empire waiting to be conquered, be it right in front of us or beyond our field of vision. While this exists, there are also unknown landscapes that can be charted with the aid of mind and reason. The role of science is absolutely essential here. Yet this profound alienation, which in the absence of reason is not somewhere afar but permeates our very selves, and which we are part and parcel of, cannot be circumscribed: despite the attempts of religion or science, one cannot elevate oneself; one remains unable to alter the vulnerability of existence. Everyone is subject to this sense of the ungraspable, whether or not they are aware of it. In moments of revelation, it is this that is reflected on the face. The face of the scientist is sober, balanced and 'composed'; yet when experiencing something beyond the boundaries of science that cannot be defined using scientific methods, its features alter; and even if it oversteps these boundaries, its previous calmness is foregone: there is nothing it could rely on in good faith. The revelation of the face in front of the unknown is not a matter of resolve; we are talking about a sense of oppression and compulsion from which no one can be exempt. It is up to us how we lead our lives—books on physiognomy base their knowledge on this, not to mention that they offer people skills based on this too. Being in possession of life is not a matter of choice: and the face, particularly in moments of passion, reveals that in the course of life the individual is subject to something that transcends life itself.

Doctors use the term 'Hippocratic face' to denote the facial features of those approaching death. Such faces emanate a benumbing tension. This is the tension between life and the absence of life, which—as a 'third' force—extends beyond both life and death: it is the unknown, the impossible in relation to which life deploys the mask-like qualities of death, and which enshrouds the petrifying face of the deceased as if it were an inaccessible and invincible existence.

Yet, the Hippocratic face is not restricted to the onset of death. It can also be spotted when, as a consequence of lightning passion, the unknown suddenly inhabits the living face. In moments of calmness, one tries to carefully steer clear of the latter as much as possible. The Chinese tend to identify this face with the all-embracing force, the manna (see Maus 1968: 28), which is impossible to pin down since it takes care of existence yet also transcends it. One does not have to wear masks in order to conjure up the unknown that cannot be oppressed: each and every live face conceals a mask—the mask of the impossible—into which existence as a whole is compressed, so that one can confront something that does not exist and yet is capable of subverting everything.

Existence tends to 'overflow' most spectacularly in the human face. When the face gets burnt from the lightning of the impossible, the *sight* in front of the *seeing* eye turns eerie. Such faces are always moving. Taking them in—be it an overjoyed child's gaze that cannot believe its eyes and gasps for air, or a face turned grey with astonishment, which is locked inward as inaccessibly as a rock—one can rightly contend that they have reached the liminal space between the sayable and the incommunicable, between bubbling vitality and deadly paralysis.

Further Thoughts on the Face

One faces the world and tries to be in denial of the unknown; by aligning their facial features, human beings make an attempt at inhibiting this on an instinctive level, too. The face is the scene of an eternal battle; it is the stage for a drama lasting from birth to death, the dramatic qualities of which are rooted in the fact that it cannot be repeated or re-enacted ever again. For this reason, every face is an adventure, and every act a mystery—from scratching to love-making and dying. A trained eye can spot a latent drama even in the most prosaic of situations, and these do not have to be spectacular events at all. When talking to someone, one tends not to pay attention to the fact that they are simultaneously conducting another conversation, and that the latter takes place without words. Psychologists use the term 'meta-communication' for this, although this is not a matter of psychological concern. This is the confrontation between one fate and another, the charged tension between faces and bodies. In the moment of 'discharge', the individual is touched by an inkling of the Other being's ultimate inaccessibility, which hints at a much deeper sense of beyond-human unfamiliarity.

In Franz Kafka's novel *The Trial*, the lawyer introduces Josef K into the secrets of his profession, as follows:

> If you look at them in the right way, the accused really can be attractive, quite often. But that is a remarkable and

to some extent scientific phenomenon [. . .] there are nonetheless those who have experience in these matters who can look at a crowd, however big, and tell you which among them is facing a charge. How can they do that, you will ask. My answer will not please you. It is simply that those who are facing a charge are the most attractive. It cannot be their guilt that makes them attractive as not all of them are guilty [. . .] and nor can it be the proper punishment that has made them attractive as not all of them are punished, so it can only be that the proceedings levelled against them take some kind of hold on them (2014: 133).

Beauty is, in a sense, also stigma: every face bears the mark of the non-human, of perfection. Beauty is moving, and not by chance; and when we are moved, every face can appear beautiful—in the moments of joy, mourning, gratification, fear, disgust, wonder, devotion or dizziness. In such moments one could perhaps talk about *distorting into beauty*: the vulnerability that has always jeopardized 'natural', 'innate' beauty comes openly to the fore in passion, and—being at odds with nature—transforms an ugly face into a beautiful one. This is the beauty of vulnerability, which is why it is not subject to the passage of time or deterioration.

By virtue of its uniqueness and drama, every face can witness the crisis of existence. This is being revealed in the lightning glance or the stiffening face. A common fate is being revealed; and this is at the root of the strange similarity among faces. The more irresistible the passion, the more impersonal the face; and it is odd that the soul is often just about to elope when the face is most enthusiastic. Beauty is impersonal and inhuman. It can transform faces into petrified lava. Looking into the passionate gaze of the Other, one realizes having had no idea what exactly was so impressive in the first place. Certainly not the eye, this gelatinous sphere, since the longer one observes it, the more lifeless it appears. Would this be the mirror of the soul? Would this inexpressive sphere, made up of connective tissue, scarfskin, nerves and water be capable of throwing lightning? The more impersonal a face, the more revealing. The eye, this impenetrable organ, does not serve the purpose of seeing. It is the sense organ of something else: the unknown, which nestles itself into the soul and turns the face and the eye astrange. In such situations, one does not see but, rather, becomes an organ of seeing, of the unknown. According to mysticism, the two eyeballs are conducting a continuous duel. The *Theologia Germanica*, attributed to the thirteenth-century Johannes Tauler, states that the soul of Christ had two eyes: with the left, he contemplated the world of creatures and time; with the right, he immersed himself in God and eternity. In the case of the created human soul, one can identify an instance of 'squinting' (*Silberblick*), with the proviso that the two eyes hinder rather than aid one another:

> [I]f the soul shall see with the right eye into eternity, then the left eye must close itself and refrain from working, and be as though it were dead. For if the left eye be fulfilling its office toward outward things; that is, holding converse with time and the creatures; then must the right eye be hindered in its working. [. . .] Therefore whosoever will have the one must let the other go; for 'no man can serve two masters' (Tauler 2016: 31).[6]

The outcome of the battle is undecided. One is at the mercy of one's own two eyes; relying on either one or the other, and hence unable to leave this inner conflict behind. It becomes apparent in the 'asymmetrical' features of the face that time and timelessness, life

---

6 In the twentieth century, it was Franz Rosenzweig who revived this thought in his work *The Star of Redemption*: 'Not that the eyes are mutually equivalent in a mimic sense, for while the left one views more receptively and evenly, the right one fixes its glance sharply on one point. Only the right one "flashes"—a division of labour which frequently leaves its mark deep in the soft neighbourhood of the eye-sockets of a hoary head; this asymmetric facial formation, which otherwise is generally conspicuous only in the familiar difference between the two profiles, then becomes perceptible also en face' (1985: 423).

and lifelessness do not exclude but presuppose one another. According to stoics, everyone is God's sense organ; yet the moments of lightning passion tell us that the face becomes emptied of God, provided he exists at all, in the very moments of this passion. What moves in is something that excludes God from the place he rightfully deserves, and transforms the human face created in God's image into a petrifying face.

Archaic Features

The passionately tense and estranged face relates the individual to ancient stone sculptures—which do not even appear to be works crafted by Man but torn from the bottom of the earth, and thus embodying everything that is not human. The faces of the archaic Greek sculptures are veiled in benumbing beauty—such statues must have been guarding Semele's palace too. This beauty deprives the individual of everything that is human within, and makes one join the fate of these silent stones. These statues are not mysterious owing to their inherent traces of feeling, passion or even supposed individualization; whoever tries to figure out their facial features can instantly become the contemporary of these statues. They drag along everyone who gets immersed in their gaze. Observing them one does not look towards the past, but recognizes oneself in their features. No statue has ever looked into the unknown with so much determination; they open up right in front of the intangible, of Nothingness. When immersing in the features of archaic sculptures, one experiences the infinite void as a personal fate; and this is why one perceives one's own being as a heavy granite block, as if lightning would strike from the faces of these statues, throwing frozen thunderbolts around themselves. Those who want to decipher the secret of these statues, instead of unmasking them, start to feel a sense of alienation from their very self. Despite their serenity, they are scarier than the later, universalized classical and Hellenistic statues. The former give commands and throw lightning; the latter, like us, are merely victims.

Petrified Lightning

The gaze throws lightning, and, in the meantime, the world of fossils looms large. Not the world of stones polished by the waves of the sea, awaiting to slide into a palm, or that of the rock carved by rain, snow or frost, but that of solidified lava. Akin to the sky cracked by lightning, solidified lava also shows the outlines of a face beyond human. Lava is just like clotted blood. Dried-out lumps protrude from it, as if recording the wounds of the earth. The earth is gravity above all; and yet, when volcanoes erupt, the earth is on an upward flight: trying to free itself from its own self. A new creation is about to begin. Fires light up from below, the nether darkness tries to transcend itself in the guise of an underground torrent of lightning. The dried-out, heavy and rock-solid bits of lava are imprints of the fire raging down below.[7] The earth did not succeed in leaving its course after all, and, in this sense, lava is also an embodiment of failure.

More than that, akin to meteorites, connected to lightning by the ancients, lava stone is the tangible copy of lightning. The spattering of lava solidifies into rock; its immovability stands for the suppression of unimaginable struggles. Lava stone is a monument of the earth besides itself, a tangible manifestation of excess. The

---

7 According to Strabo, 'midway between Thera and Therasia flames rushed forth from the sea for the space of four days; causing the whole of it to boil and be all on fire; and after a little an island twelve stadia in circumference, composed of the burning mass, as thrown up, as if raised by machinery' (*Geography* 1.3.16). The creation of this island was attributed to Poseidon; the trident, the weapon of this earthly-underwordly god was initially joined together from three bolts of lightning. Understandably, several volcanoes were sites of religious rites; and akin to the ancient Jews who threw their children into the fire to honour Moloch, volcanoes have also regularly devoured their human victims (see Frazer 1963: 191).

impossible is embodied in it—something beyond description or perception, something that does not allow anything to identify with itself, and which cannot be called 'that', at most THAT, THAT IS NOT THAT. Akin to the crater, a visible facet of universal chaos, this eyeball of the earth reminiscent of the wound, lava stone is a messenger of an all-subversive struggle. Existence made an attempt at breaking out of itself in the course of a lightning torrent of fire, and the impossible emerged under the guise of rough solidifying rock. Everything that there is, and is understandable and possible, is a guise of this impossible. Everything that exists owes their birth to something that, as a unique lightning beyond the earth and the sky, cracks open what hitherto did not exist, and, by subverting it, fashions it into something existent.

Who Lightens? (Who Flashes with Lightning?)

Is it possible to attribute a subject to this verb? The answer seems obvious: the lightning lightens; to be precise, it flashes with lightning. But this is misleading. It seems to suggest that lightning exists, and that it tends to emit occasional flashes of light and then withdraws to its hideaway. In other words, lightning 'as such' does exist, even prior to it allowing to be seen, following which it emits the visible bolts of lightning, the 'lightning phenomena'. This hypothesis is reminiscent of the classic idea that people have a 'subconscious', a 'repository' that is always available and accessible, and it is up to the conscious to select, as and when, what is required from this stock. Based on empirical data, however, the relationship between these two poles is rather different, despite obvious differences between the unconscious and the conscious; and it is the previously-mapped-out analogy between the pronounceable and the unpronounceable that proves to be helpful in this context too. It is not the conscious that gets inspiration from the unconscious as it sees fit, gradually decreasing its scale (in a utopia this would lead to the complete liquidation of the subconscious and the absolute dominance of the conscious), but the conscious that gives birth to the unconscious, following which there is a proportionate increase in both. Using a daring analogy, this is also applicable to the case of lightning. We cannot really talk about lightning 'as such' until it appears in the sky; but it is not accurate to say that lightning only manifests itself 'as a phenomenon'. Lightning does not exist 'in itself'; the light of lightning hints at something that is beyond it, despite the fact that, strictly speaking, there is Nothing beyond it at all. There is no thunder without sound and no rain without raindrops, so there is no lightning without the light of lightning either. When lightning cracks the sky open for a moment, it seems as if the world will break out of itself and squeeze into the gap, through which, as if through an eye socket, it will contemplate itself.

Who lightens therefore?

In the midst of lightning, one has the impression as if creation was about to begin anew. Thinking of the moments of creation, however, one cannot talk about action and event, subject and predicate. Lightning is situated beyond all measure; therefore, also beyond any measurable differentiation between subject and predicate. Such things are only imaginable in a world already created and solidified into existence.

Consequently, could it be that the lightning of creation is uncreated?

According to relevant mythologies shared by several cultures, lightning is the weapon of the chief god—Zeus in the case of Greeks. It is natural that he is the one throwing the bolts of lightning; in other words, he is the one that lightens. Using an awkward turn of the phrase: he is the one that 'makes lightning happen'. Lightning was put together and handed over to Zeus by the Cyclopes, children of Gaia, the Earth: Brontes (thunder), Steropes (lightning) and Arges (brightness) (Hesiod 1914: 141). Thus, aided by lightning, Earth and Sky are joined together; and lightning unites these two extremes. The three Cyclopes have not only forged lightning but, as their name reveals, also embodied it: 'the winds brought rumbling earthquake and duststorm, thunder (*brontén*), and lightning (*steropén*) and the lurid thunderbolt (*aithaloenta keraunos*)', Hesiod notes (ibid.: 689–94). It would appear from this as if lightning, this force aiming to prevent all separation, were characterized by a dual nature: on the one hand, object (the weapon of Zeus), and on the other, force (also proven by the fact that lightning—in fact, Keraunos, thunderbolt—had been honoured as a god in his own right until sixth century BCE).

If we pay close attention to the character of Zeus, and to his name in particular, it emerges that the weapon in his possession could only be so effective because it had benefitted from his godliness. The name Zeus was derived by adding *u* (dieus) to the Indo-German root *dei-, deiə-, dī-, diū* (or *diā*?), connected to brightness and gleaming light (Pokorny 1959: 183–5). The name of the god denotes a light homogenous with lightning. 'From Heaven and from Olympus he (Zeus) came forthwith, hurling his lightning,' Hesiod observes (1914: 689–90). Lightning originating on Mount Olympus is not a mere element in the atmosphere. The name of the mountain (*Hololampé* = shining through) is an allusion to the absence of storms. In Homer's words: Olympus 'is the abode of the gods that stands fast forever. Neither is it shaken by winds nor ever wet with rain, nor does snow fall upon it, but the air is outspread clear and cloudless, an over it hovers a radiant whiteness' (*Odyssey* 4.42–5).

Lightning associated with a god does not emerge from the friction of clouds but from glare. This glare embodies Zeus himself. In order to make his might visible, the chief god has to throw lightning; yet this would not reach its goal if in the exact moment he would not also strike in person, in the shape of lightning. Thus, lightning is weapon (object) and live force (subject) at the same time.

Having such a 'dual' nature, how can lightning be nevertheless unified (unifying)? Examining the name further helps us resolve this problem. The name derived from the Indo-Germanic root is not only related to light but also to life: the terms *zóé* = life, *zóó* = to live, and *zóos* = living are also connected to the name of the god, whose occasional name in dialect is: Zén, which is related to the verb 'to live'. Thus, it is the intimate relationship between life and light that emerges, also underpinned by Homer: 'to go on living and see the light of the sun' (*Iliad* 24.558; see Heidegger 1954: 274). In this way, lightning is not only a manifestation of earthly or heavenly light but also that of life itself, which unites the earthly and heavenly worlds despite their differences. (The Greeks utilized the noun *óon* [living being] in relation to both animals and gods: Animals, people and gods are similar in that they are all living beings. All three partake of the same life, which suggests that life, despite being unimaginable without them, also transcends them: they are in the service of something that can only manifest through and by them.)

The unity of life and light is embodied by many other things in addition to lightning. Let us turn to the sun, for instance, and its invigorating rays. Not only does lightning revitalize and illuminate, but it also destroys; it can ruin life itself. Is this compatible with a chief god? And if so, why with him above all others?

Examining this god's name further we find that the name Zeus conceals an additional meaning that points beyond light and life, and reminds us of the most characteristic features of this god. The Greeks derived their intensifier, the meaning of which is *very*, from a variant of the word *zóós* (living): *zós*. They would have utilized this term in relation to gods, too; the tragedians or Pindar did not label as saint something that was simply divine, but what was 'very divine'. '*En zatheó . . . chronó*'—'in the holy (very divine) times', Pindar observes about an era in which he summons the gods with the express aim to prophesize (*Paeans* 6.5); '*zatheos hieron*'—'very divine holy place', he notes, aiming to lay emphasis on the holiness of a church (ibid.: fr. 105).

The adjectives 'living' and 'bright' convey characteristics; they are usually assigned to qualify something. But is it possible to assign adjectives to God? Can we ascribe adjectives to things on which the very existence of these characteristics is dependant? Can we call something wise, kind or just when they are in fact a precondition of wisdom, kindness or justice? What we tend to call divine cannot be compared or measured; yet the wise, the kind and the just can only be wise, kind and just if considered in relation to something else.

The intensifier 'very' illustrates this fact. We cannot consider Zeus alive, because he is life itself; we cannot call him bright, because he is light. Neither of the latter can be intensified: life cannot be more alive, light cannot be brighter. And because both emanate from Zeus, they cannot be called life or light either: life as well as light are both divine, but God himself is neither life nor light. In the words of Dionysius the Areopagite, God is non-existent and not non-existent at the same time: he is above everything. The term 'very' conveys this inaccessibility and incommensurability. Much later, in the ninth century, Scotus Erigena noted, not about Zeus but God, that one has to add 'very' (*nimis*) to the list of adjectives assigned to God because this is the only way to convey that 'God exceeds every measure' (*Periphyseon* 2.28). In this sense, the name Zeus is most accurate: the intensification inherent in his name (Very) makes the use of adjectival constructs redundant. Lightning exceeds everything as if it were God, and it is very difficult to characterize or describe what actually appears in the moment of lightning. This would lead to a linguistic absurdity on a par with the use of the term 'very' as a noun in its own right.

The Matrix of Existence

And yet, if we were to ask the question anew, who lightens, that is who flashes with lightning, the only answer is: the VERY. When the sky tears open, it is the VERY that glances into existence through the root-like cracks. This same glance lightens in every earthly gaze too: in such moments it is not only passion that flashes up in the eye but also, as the source of all passion, the VERY. Each and every being is at the mercy of this. It does not lie low in faraway hiding places (such as darkness, the subconscious or the unspeakable) but is nascent in the moments of passion (the silver flash, the divine experience). These are the moments of self-discovery. One experiences oneself as identical with oneself in such moments—while the experience of being different from one's self has never been more obvious. Lightning is simultaneously weapon and God, object and subject. Lightning does not only illuminate the world, the latter also becomes enlightened and fulfilled through the former. It turns out in such situations that VERY is the connective tissue of existence—something that cannot be articulated, qualified or enclosed into adjectival constructs. Hölderlin's 'Revealed' hints at the impossibility to circumscribe lightning, the 'divine fire', and in moments of enlightenment, when one finds one's own self without being able to trace this back to a tangible reason. In such situations one partakes of a 'divine experience'—although one could also rightly claim to have found oneself in the impossible.

The Everlasting Fire

'Very'. It is impossible to pin down what this term really means. The word, the task of which would be to intensify the meaning of other words, appears incomplete on its own. Yet it retains its role as an intensifier and, for lack of a better context, starts to intensify the sense of absence that feeds on its incompleteness. The substantival variant of the word not to be used on its own is the manifestation of barrenness and uselessness. The more it strives for independence, the more intrusive the absence spreading therein and around.

This absence is not Nothingness, though; it is a kind of enlightenment. Pure glare, blinding light illuminate existence—the light that, according to mythology, administers life and decay, self-discovery and self-emptying. Pindar compares lightning and thunder to everlasting fire (*Pythian* 1.5). This fire permeates existence, the seen and the unseen;[8] this is what turns burning hot during moments of passion and shock; this offers the experience of the impossible; this cracks the sky open; this crystallizes into blood-clot-like lava stones; and this distorts, akin to a mysterious mask, the face and, eerily, the light.

In the moments when VERY manifests itself, one partakes in the specificity of lightning. It transforms into an abandoned intensifier, left to its own devices, into an exclusive VERY. It perceives life as a crack, wedged into the unknown prior to birth and following death. The individual is inclined to believe that one is flashing with lightning, too. One facet of their self urges them to move on and contemplate the 'Revealed' evoked by Hölderlin; the other, however, knows full well that self-revelation has already happened.

---

8 In the *Iliad*, Homer named Pluto, living under the earth, as 'the Zeus of the Underworld', which could also be translated as glare in eternal darkness (1898: 457).

CHAPTER 3

THE MYSTERY OF THE NAVEL

Titian, *The Flaying of Marsyas*

Vitruvius composed the ideal and harmonious body according to the principles of the golden ratio: around a man standing with legs wide apart and hands stretched out, he drew a circle, the centre of which was the body's navel. Several others joined him in this approach: the likes of Leonardo, Agrippa von Nettesheim, Cesare Cesarino, Dürer, Le Corbusier, and the navel has gradually emerged as the symbol of the centre, of proportion and of harmony.

By making it to the centre—or, rather, by becoming the centre—doesn't one, however, break away from one's surroundings? Can we talk of perfect harmony in situations where discord is excluded? The geometrical centre of Titian's last painting is also a navel: the navel of a 'man', a satyr hanging from his feet, who is about to be skinned by Apollo surrounded by bloodthirsty acolytes. The navel symbolizes the vulnerability of the powerlessly revealing body, and, in the event of any further stretches of the body, this is the point whereby everything enclosed into the darkness within would find its outward passage. The navel is the mark of mortality, and the very centre through which everything that exists attempts to recognize its own intended purpose.

'The body is capable of a degree of tension, fragmentation, density, and impenetrability that surpasses all philosophy, dialectics, music, physics, poetry, and magic', Antonin Artaud contended shortly before his death in his lecture 'Theatre and Science'. Seeing his audience's seeming incomprehension, he added: 'I would have had to shit blood through my navel in order to make myself understood and to arrive at what I wanted' (Artaud 1965: 169–73).

When Epimenides visited the Oracle of Delphi in sixth century BCE, the prophetess Pythia was not faced with an average caller. The man from Crete had been surrounded by legendary fame already in his lifetime, and rumour has it that as a young man he fell asleep in the shadow of a cave while shepherding, and when he woke up his herd was nowhere to be seen. He returned to his village in a hurry but was greeted by people unfamiliar to him, and no one recognized him either. Finally, he came across a white-haired old man in whom he was surprised to find his own younger brother. The latter informed him that he had been asleep in the cave for 57 years. Later it started to dawn on him that he had spent these years in the company of gods, since the cave in which he lay down was none other than the cave of Zeus on Mount Ida.[1] Epimenides learnt everything from the gods that was true and just; and thus he acquired a mysterious knowledge attested by both his acclaimed books and his subsequent reputation as a doctor.

---

1 Pythagoras visited this same cave at a later point, aiming to cleanse and enlighten himself.

The Oracle of Delphi, where Apollo 'chants to men, and priests interpret present and predict future events' (Euripides, *Ion* 3), was visited by a man who, having spent time with the gods, had some idea of the present and future. Yet he found the prophetess's guidance vague and ambivalent (Plutarch, *De defectu* 409), which may have led to his disappointment when he made the following, to other ears equally vague and ambivalent, claim: 'There was no Omphalos, either in the centre of the earth or of the sea. If any there be, it is visible to the gods, not visible to mortals' (DK 3B11; Freeman 1983[1948] trans.).

Epimenides' words are clearly bitter, as if it were not just earthly beings who are cursed—the latter by their lack of immortality and heavenly beings by their lack of mortality. Could this mutual lack constitute the true navel of the earth, this fatal crack that emerges from time to time, like the scales of a serpent creeping up from the dark to the warming rays of the sun? But more of the serpent anon.

Light and Rot

Let us conjure up mythological descriptions on the navel of the earth. Zeus wanted to know where the centre of the Earth was; so he set two eagles off, flying at equal speed, one eastbound and the other westbound, to see where they would meet. The two birds touched down in Delphi, where this was commemorated with a white stone pillar rounded off at the top, the *omphalos*. The meaning of this word is 'navel'. The oracle established there was considered the centre of the Earth, and has been known as the navel of the Earth for centuries (Strabo, *Geography* 9.3.5).[2]

---

2 Plutarch tells us in first century CE that two men set off from the opposite ends of the (then) inhabited Earth: the grammarian Demetrius from present-day England, and the Spartan Cleombrotos from the Persian Gulf, only to meet in Delphi, too (*De defectu*, 410a).

The navel of the Earth is right in the centre by virtue of its location—neither in the east, west, north or south. It is a no man's land in the mould of the petrifying Gorgon's hut, bordering on both east and west and untouched by the light of the Sun or the Moon. The navel of the Earth absorbs the cardinal points, not to mention time—thus facilitating prophecy, just as the Gorgon's home absorbs light. Akin to a 'black hole', it draws everything in, and devours like a predator all those who venture too close by. On the slopes of Parnassus near Delphi there was an abyss-like cave, inhabited since times immemorial by a giant serpent, the mighty Python. This enormous puffed-up wild beast would not only prey on locals but also block the road leading to the oracle (Apollodorus, *The Library* 1.4.1). Apollo, the son of Zeus, who had previously 'civilized the peoples [. . . by way of cultivating] fruits and life' (Strabo, *Geography* 9.3.12), proved to be of help on this occasion too and set off towards Parnassus. With his arrow, he killed the serpent and took possession of the oracle. 'The oracle is in a hollow cave that is deep with a rather narrow mouth, and from which a divinely inspired breath rises up,' geographer Strabo writes. 'A high tripod is placed over the mouth which the Pythia mounts and, receiving the breath, utters both metrical and unmetrical oracles' (*Geography* 9.3.5).

An explanation for the steam taking to the air from below the Earth was provided by the rotting body of the serpent (*pythein* = to rot), and the prophetesses inhaling this steam were thus named Pythias.[3] The serpent, however, had already been emanating such a rotting smell in its lifetime (and this made the prophetesses experience a state of ecstasy), not to mention that its very birth was also due to rot,[4] which is why it is more plausible to associate Python's

---

3 Strabo wrongly originates their name in the verb '*pythesthai*' (to ask about) (*Geography* 9.3.5).

4 'When Earth, spread over with diluvian ooze, felt heat ethereal from the glowing sun,
  unnumbered species to the light she gave,

name with depth (rather than decay) and with the words *pythmen*, *bythos* = foundation, base, bottom, depth (*Paulys Realencyclopädie* 1963: 517–18). Despite the fact that Pythia was the priestess of Sun (Apollo) and light, she could only be inspired by the night and the light of the Moon. To put it differently, the God of light from above would end up delivering their prophecy by descending into the darkness below. The Greeks founded the oracle at the very site where the Earth cracked open in the shape of a cave, thus incorporating the unearthly and giving off the underwordly.

The body of the Earth cracks open. A wound opens wherein height and depth, east and west, light and darkness connect in a single centre, ground zero and *origo*: the navel.

The Sutured Wound

A stone pillar marks the navel of the Earth, the *omphalos*, which is located neither to the right, nor to the left, front, back, above or below. It seems as if the world would turn inside out at this meeting point of mysterious forces. This is where superior knowledge (prophecy) meets ecstasy (Pythia), cruelty (the massacre of Python), expiation (according to some, Apollo was subjected to regular penitence for his killing of Python), even despair (Epimenides). It is also an enigmatic point that attracts everything like a magnet.

The navel of the Earth is a sutured wound, the opening of which could instantly reveal the underlying depth. It is here that existence thickens; and where everything that the individual associates with one's own centre braids together. Exploring this centre appears as the most urgent of needs; however, upon finding it in Delphi, 'in the prophesying navel of the Earth', one is also confronted with

---

and gave to being many an ancient form,
or monster new created. Unwilling she
created thus enormous Python.' (Ovid, *Metamorphoses* 1.434–40)

various tensions all too difficult to release. At times, avoiding these promises to be a more comforting option, even if this means giving up on the centre itself. Yet, it is impossible to resist the appeal of the centre for good, and ultimately we end up obeying it even in our death.[5]

The Nest of Vitality

Why the navel? Why not the heart, the liver, the gall, the brain, the genitals? Why does the Greek *omphalos*, the Sanskrit *nabhi* and the Tibetan *lte-ba*, in addition to 'navel', also mean centre and nucleus? And why is the human body at the foundation of this analogy?

A piece of writing by Hippocrates helps to answer these questions. The Greeks did not only deem Delphi as the navel of the Earth:

---

5 Delphi is not the only navel of the Earth. To be precise, the Earth has a single navel but this 'migrates': appearing wherever it is needed. After all, we are not dealing with a specific point in space, since the navel transcends and even overtakes space. The Egyptians thought of the holy mountain used as an oracle for the sun god Ompha-el as a navel; the Phoenicians considered Paphos on the island of Cyprus as the navel of the Earth, and there was an oracle here too, complete with a temple for Apollo; according to Ezekiel, Israel is the centre of the world and Jerusalem 'the midst of the land' (Ezekiel 38:12), more specifically the hilt of the cross placed on the site of the tree of life, where if one stuck a rod into the ground it would cast no shadow at noon; and in Palestine they considered Mount Thabor a navel (*tabbûr* = navel; Eliade 1969: 25). Other nations also marked the navel of the Earth, such as the Arabs, the Romans (the round hearth of the Vesta temple in Rome), the Sicilians (the town of Enna), the Hungarians (Naszály near Tata), the Celts, the Scandinavians (they called their country Midgard, the centre of the Earth), the Japanese, the Malaysians, the Babylonians, the Incas (the capital, Cuzco), the Aztecs, the Chinese (the city of Loyang, and the imperial palace), the Buryats, the Finnish, the Pueblo Indians (they offered sacrifices to all four cardinal points, as well as the zenith and nadir, but held the navel in the highest regard), the Tibetans (lte-ba gzhung-rang is the name of the palace where the Dalai Lama lives—this translates as 'the navel of its own centre'), and the Indians (Meru, the golden mountain guarded by snakes, and Gaya Magadha, where Buddha became enlightened).

they also considered the island of the nymph Calypso 'where is the navel of the sea' (Homer, *Odyssey* 1.51), the town of Phlius, as well as Branchos (Didyma) in Miletus, which has been in an age-long competition with the Oracle of Delphi over precedence and fame. The sixth-century author of a Hippocratic writing about the number seven labels Miletus and the whole of Ionia the *diaphragm* of the Earth (*frenos–praecordia*), following the archaic thought that the human body and the cosmos are not only constructed in similar ways (Roscher 1913: 39) but are also in a correlation and share deep-rooted similarities. A point of view connected to Hippocrates and based on the theory of liquids started off with the idea of amalgamation departing from the body and arrived at a vision comprising the entire cosmos and the position of the planets. By contrast, a school of thought privileging a cosmic standpoint arrived at scrutinizing the human body following the examination of the cosmos and the introduction of the four elements—earth, water, fire, air—first mentioned by Empedocles, also known as a healer. In this way, empirical liquids gain cosmic, and cosmic elements empirical significance.

It is particularly revealing to consider references to the 'diaphragm' (*frenos*) in relation to the Oracle of Branchos known as the navel of the Earth. The author of this treatise wanted to emphasize in this way the central role of Ionia in contemporary civilization. The Greeks did not only consider the diaphragm the centre of the body but also the seat of the soul and thought.[6] *Frenos*

6 Much later, in the tenth century, Simeon the New Theologian writes the followings in his treatise, *Method of Holy Prayer and Attention*: 'Then seat yourself in a quiet cell, apart in a corner, and apply yourself to doing as I shall say: close the door, raise your mind above any vain or transitory object. Then, pressing your beard against your chest, direct the eye of the body and with all your mind upon the center of your belly—that is, upon your navel—compress the inspiration of air passing through the nose so that you do not breathe easily, and mentally examine the interior of your entrails in search of the place of the heart, where all the powers of the soul delight to linger. In the beginning,

means diaphragm *and* feeling, intellect, soul, spirit, temper, talent (frantic = manic, mad, distraught). Hippocrates himself would have utilized the terms diaphragm and navel, i.e. *omphalos*, as synonyms because they are not only located in each other's vicinity but also carry out a similarly distinctive role. Fifth-century BCE Pythagorean scholar Philolaos postulated that the navel was one of the four roots of Man, in addition to the head, heart and genitals (DK 44B13), thus following Democritus: 'The navel forms first in the womb, as an anchorage against tossing and wandering, a cable and a rope for the fruit, engendered and future' (DK 68B148; Freeman 1983[1948] trans.). (*Omphalos* meant both navel and umbilical cord.)

According to this position, the navel gains not so much a geometrical but a physiological and genealogical importance. The seventeenth-century physician Sir Thomas Browne describes in his work *Pseudodoxia Epidemica* that Adam and Eve could not have had navels since they were not born but given life by God. Their descendants, by contrast, could legitimately have navels, because although they also existed by virtue of God's grace, they were situ-ated at a considerably lower level of the creation process (Browne 1964a: 5.5).[7] The umbilical cord symbolizes being created; it is life's channel in that it connects the foetus with the mother, and ensures that something that does not yet exist can become Something. The

you will find darkness and stubborn opacity, but if you persevere, if you prac-tice this exercise day and night, you will find—O, wonder!—a boundless felicity' (quoted in Eliade 1958: 64–5).

7 James Joyce revives this idea in *Ulysses*: 'Spouse and helpmate of Adam Kadmon: Heva, naked Eve. She had no navel. Gaze. Belly without blemish, bulging big, a buckler of taut vellum, no, whiteheaped corn, orient and immortal, standing from everlasting to everlasting. Womb of sin' (1986[1922]: 31). Browne's views were rebutted in the nineteenth century on the basis of natural history and the theory of evolution by Philip Henry Gosse, in his work *Omphalos: An Attempt to Untie the Geological Knot* (1857). Gosse argued that nature has an indisputable history, from where ensues that creation did not take place in time but was a 'prochronic' event (1857: 336).

navel is an indication of life (according to the indigenous population of the Antilles, only the dead have no navels), and this is the reason for its magic powers: this is the point where everything that, according to Hippocrates, distinguishes the diaphragm (soul, spirit, temper, etc.) accesses Man, and upon death, departs therefrom. The umbilical cord, a remnant of which is the navel knot, was venerated on this account in a variety of cultures: in Polynesia the umbilical cords of newborn babies were interred and trees planted above, these trees being perceived as these individuals' tree of life (Roscher 1913: 13); in Uganda the king's umbilical cord was kept in a dedicated temple and considered as the ruler's 'external soul' (Frazer 1963: 147); and the umbilical cord was preserved by the Japanese, the Incas and the Germans, too. It was met everywhere with the veneration manifested by the Greeks towards chief God Zeus' umbilical cord, which was thought to have dropped off soon after the God's birth in the vicinity of Cnossus, following which that land became known as Omphalion by the inhabitans of Cydon (Callimachus, *Hymns 1: To Zeus* 45–6).[8]

On the Nature of the Serpent

Before we return to the navel of the Earth, let us pause for a moment at the shape of the serpent. Had Python, the dragon serpent that stayed behind after the flood, not resided under the Earth, Apollo would not have come to Delphi, and neither would the oracle been founded. Without the serpent and the rotting smell pouring out from below, mortals would not have managed to get the God of light to start a conversation with them. Serpents thrive in crevices and cracks; and the Earth is the realm of invisible depth and obscurity, which humans are afraid of. Ancient notions are associated

---

8 According to widespread Hindu custom, prior to building a house one would place a snakeskin under its foundation, thus making the new construction point towards 'the centre of the world' (Mundkur 1983: 276).

with it; as if creation has been engendered by it, only for its barrel-shaped body, akin to the wide-open hungry mouth of the dragon serpent seen in the painting *Saint Margaret* attributed to Raphael, to reclaim what it has previously given off. 'The outer darkness is a great dragon,' Jesus contends in the Gnostic writing *Pistis Sophia: A Gnostic Miscellany*, 'with its tail in its mouth; it is outside the world (cosmos) and surroundeth it completely' (1905: chap. 126). The serpent embodies the universal principle of creation, and chooses to attack creation upon its most sensitive point—its navel, where confusion could transform into order, and chaos into cosmos. This is the reason why the serpent biting its own tail has come to symbolize the cyclicality of creation, as existence folds into itself and finds fulfilment in the shape of the serpent (Leisegang 1985: 111).[9] Wherever it appears, the serpent generates fear; it embodies the foreign, the Other, the untouchable—something that fills the human being with disgust and ensures that one does not venture too close to it.[10]

Examining the remarkable role of the serpent in psychoanalysis, Carl Gustav Jung took note of all contradictory mythological (especially Christian) notions,[11] and concluded that the serpent is situated

---

9 This is why oracles have a predilection for serpents, and Pythia herself is often represented holding a serpent over her knee. The cult of the serpent is among the most ancient rituals across the world (see Mundkur 1983: 6; Raulff 1988: 78–9).

10 Carl Gustav Jung calls attention to the fact that the Sethian sect of the Gnostics identified the cerebrum (*encephalon*) with the Father, and the cerebellum and the bone marrow (*parencephalis draconteides—dracon* = dragon serpent!) with the Son. Jung therefore concluded that 'the snake does in fact symbolize "cold-blooded", inhuman contents and tendencies of an abstractly intellectual as well as a concretely animal nature: in a word, the extra-human quality in man' (1970: 186).

11 When people started to speak against God, he sent fiery serpents upon them (4 Moses 21:6); yet it was the Lord who instructed Moses to forge a fiery copper serpent, the sight of which would save the life of everyone who is bitten

at the centre of a mythical system of power, the four poles of which
are actively engaged in each and every human being.[12] These poles
are Christ, the Devil, the Nascent Being (*rotundum*) and the Being
Descending into Nature (*anthropos*). Thus, the serpent represents
the strongest possible contradiction and tension, one that the individual is unable to bear; for this reason, it is transposed into the
unconscious. As a result, the serpent also becomes a symbol of
human vulnerability: the embodiment of weakness and the unconscious (Jung 1970: 186).

One does one's best to protect oneself from everything that
could seriously hit home; which is why one labels excess, disgust and

---

(4 Moses 21:8). Satan appears in the shape of a serpent, yet John likens Christ
to it: 'And as Moses lifted up the serpent in the wilderness, even so must the
Son of man be lifted up' (John 3:14).

12 The utmost level in yoga meditation is the so-called *samyama*, a moment
whereby the yogi is in full control over their body and soul, and conscious
of everything that has hitherto been left unconscious (Eliade 1958: 70).
According to classical yoga philosopher Patanjali, depending on what
samyama focuses on, Man can acquire extraordinary qualities; in this context
he mentions in particular the navel area, the umbilical plexus (*nabhi-chakra*),
the examination of which can reveal the entire system of the human body.
The navel area is one of the body's seven chakras (Sanskrit term for wheel),
or seven vortexes of energy, which form a system of energy ranging from the
lowest point between the genitals and the anus, to the highest point situated
at the upper left part of the brain. In order to accede to the utmost level in
meditation, all dormant energy vortexes need to be revitalized. This role is
bestowed upon the serpent-shaped Kundalini, a source of ur-energy that lies
dormant coiled up in the nether regions of the body, which, if awoken, creeps
up through all the seven chakras, bringing them back to life. Yogis awaken
the Kundalini serpent with the aid of breathing and physical exercises, following which more complex tasks are performed to get it up to the last chakra
situated at the very top. Owing to its fiery nature, Tantric Buddhism has
declared the navel area, the seat of eternal fire, as the fitting home to this serpent; and it is from here that it rises to move along the chakras in order to
finally reach—according to a Buddhist poem—(through the navel of the
Earth) the peak of Mount Meru (the centre or axis of the world, guarded by
serpents) and ascend to the heavens (ibid.: 246).

the appalling as 'evil'. This is rooted in the innate conviction that what can be named can also be kept at bay. Yet whenever the individual is heading towards its own centre, one is forced to acknowledge the fact that excess cannot be constrained by boundaries, that it simply shows up everywhere. One is in a position of locating one's own centre whenever one can find oneself in something that permeates everything and appears in everything, and in this way also holds everything together. The navel of the Earth in mythological descriptions is the abode of the serpent, the centre beyond space and time: yet all this is but a tame image and metaphor intended to convey the inconceivable, the unutterable and the all-subversive. One summons one's opponent, the light-radiating redeemer, and the serpent dwelling in darkness in order to avoid confronting the impossible, and to ensure that one always sees 'Something' in front of one's eyes. One labels the former harmful and the latter creative, yet they are part of one and the same vortex. This vortex is the site and moment of the often-evoked divine experience.

The Mouth of the Earth

When examining the navel of the Earth, references to the cosmogony of the Sethian Gnostic sect can be highly informative. Akin to other sects (Ophites, the Naaseni), they also dedicated particular attention to the serpent, teaching the followings: 'Now of principles, he says, the substances are light and darkness; and of these, spirit is intermediate without admixture [. . .]. The heaven and the earth have a figure similar to the womb, having a navel in the midst'. The next step is impregnation, in which the serpent also assumes a role:

> For he (a perfect mind) was a ray (sent down) from above,
> from that perfect light, (and) was overpowered in the dark,
> and formidable, and bitter, and defiled water; and he is a
> luminous spirit borne down over the water. But the wind,
> at the same time fierce and formidable, whirling along, is,

in respect of its hissing sound, like a serpent. First, then, from the wind—that is, from the serpent—has resulted the originating principle of generation in the manner declared, all things having simultaneously received the principle of generatio. After, then, the light and the spirit had been received, he says, into the polluted and baneful (and) dis- ordered womb, the serpent—the wind of the darkness, the first-begotten of the waters—enters within and produces man (Hyppolitus, *Against All Heresies* 5.14).[13]

According to this view, the world can be perceived as an enor- mous womb. Down below is the simmering chaos, above is the light, and the two are connected by the phallic serpent. The serpent embodies light and logos, but also the navel and the umbilical cord.

---

13 Third-century scholar Hyppolitus, who recorded Sethian cosmogony, con- tends the following on his Gnostic opponents:

> The entire system of their doctrine, however, is (derived) from the ancient theologians Musaeus, and Linus, and Orpheus, who eluci- dates especially the ceremonies of initiation, as well as the mysteries themselves. For their doctrine concerning the womb is also the tenet of Orpheus; and the (idea of the) navel, which is harmony, is (to be found) with the same symbolism attached to it in the Bacchanalian orgies of Orpheus. But prior to the observance of the mystic rite of Celeus, and Triptolemus, and Ceres, and Proserpine, and Bacchus in Eleusis, these orgies have been celebrated and handed down to men in Phlium of Attica. For antecedent to the Eleusinian mysteries, there are (enacted) in Phlium the orgies of her denominated the Great (Mother). There is, however, a portico in this (city), and on the portico is inscribed a representation, (visible) up to the present day, of all the words which are spoken (on such occasions). [. . .] And in the greater number of these books is also drawn the repre- sentation of a certain aged man, grey-haired, winged, having his pudendum erectum, pursuing a retreating woman of azure colour. And over the aged man is the inscription 'phaos ruentes' (*Against All Heresies* 5.145).

The umbilical cord connecting the foetus (the sky) and the maternal womb (the Earth) is also a phallus with which the sky impregnates the Earth.

The realms of the above and the below are in contact through the medium of the navel; and 'harmony' is created as a result of cosmic union.[14] This theory of creation explains the cosmic nature of Delphi and its oracle-like navel. The name Delphi is connected to the Greek term for womb (*delphys* = womb, uterus). The cave inhabited by Python (also known as Delphyne) was known to the Greeks as the mouth of the Earth: *stoma*, or *stomaion*. S*toma*, however, does not only mean mouth: it can also mean navel (see Liddell and Scott 1843: *Stoma* keyword), but more frequently it means female genitals—vagina (Delcourte 1955: 141). 'And you who occupy the mighty, gorgeously built cavern,' the chorus addresses Apollo in Aeschylus' tragedy *The Libation Bearers* (806). This could also be translated as: 'You who, as sun god and divine *phallos*, blissfully enter the womb down below through the labia of the Earth.'

The navel of the Earth: the site for the interpenetration of light from above and darkness from below, the intercourse of Heaven and Earth revealed in the moment of orgasm. *Nabh*, the Sanskrit term at the root of the word *omphalos*, also means tearing, laceration, crack. The navel is the point where something cracks open, where the body opens along a 'wound' (such as the vagina), and where—to cite Epimenides—the visible becomes invisible and the invisible visible.

The cave into which those visiting the Oracle of Delphi descended leads to the stomach of the Earth, the kingdom of darkness. It is telling that Apollo's first temple in Delphi was built by the same Trophonios whose cave in Lebadea later came to symbolize hopelessness. In this cave one had the chance to experience the prophecies of Trophonios, at times venerated as Zeus; however, no

---

14 According to Indian mythology, the very first man was ritually dismembered, with the head representing the heavens, the feet the Earth, and the navel the atmosphere. The term *omphalos* also has a (largely unfounded) meaning which connects it to the phallus, partly due to the phallic shape of the navel stone.

one who ever visited this place was able to smile again. Legend has it that Christ had also opened up a cave for Saint Patrick on the Irish island of Lough Dergen, in which those who spent a whole night and day could encounter the full scale of torments and delights in store in Hell and Heaven. In other words, they were initiated into the mysteries of the impossible. Those visiting the caves in Lebadea or Delphi must have partaken of similar experiences.[15] The prophecy of the unknown, of the womb of the Earth, is just as alluring as the song of the sirens, yet its fulfilment can easily lead to despair—since in the process it is none other than the *womb* of existence, or, rather, being itself, that starts to come into view.

The Intemperance of the Centre

One of Apollo's many names is the Pythian. The God of light not only descends into darkness and decay but also partakes of the latter's qualities. He exposes himself to danger in the same way as his priestess Pythia, whose rapture was explained by Strabo with an underwordly gust of wind (*Geography* 9.3.5). The geographer talks about *pneuma enthusiasticon*—inspiring steam, hinting at the dangers facing Pythia. Plutarch contends that a bad whiff (*pneuma*) could even cause the priestess's death (*De defectu* 438b–c). Elation and enthusiasm could become so excessive that, under the influence of divine gust, the priestess would fall into ecstasy and frenzy. In states of ecstasy, one is beside oneself (*ek-histanai* = displaced), and the space left 'empty' is occupied by chaos. Could it be though that it was chaos itself that displaced the individual from its 'original' position?

---

15 The depth of the Earth was enticing prophecy in many parts of the world: on the island of Madagascar, the prophet Ramahavaly (the One Who Can Answer) lived in a secret cave, where he not only prophesied but also acted as the patron of serpents (!) (see Pennick 1979: 46).

The navel of the Earth is also the seat of chaos. Prior to the arrival of Apollo, the God of light and moderation, other gods would have been offered sacrifices at Delphi. Dionysius first of all, since 'the people of Delphi believe that the remains of Dionysus rest with them close beside the oracle; and the Holy Ones offer a secret sacrifice in the shrine of Apollo' (Plutarch, *Isis and Osiris* 35). This connection to a tortured and lacerated God associates the navel of the Earth with the orgastic. In fact, Apollo had to share his power with Dionysius from the very beginning: and as light mingled with obscurity, and brightness with simmering decay, reason had to give way to intoxication, and unity had to tolerate rupture. Nietzsche's later concepts of the Apollonian and the Dionysian were braided together in a self-evident fashion at the Oracle of Delphi, yet this in no way obscured their differences and dialectical synthesis. On the contrary: the emerging tension reached the pinnacle of endurability here in the centre. Making it to the navel of the Earth, the individual turns into a being akin to a navel and, serving as the very intersection of opposites, becomes the place where the world finds its own centre.[16] In such situations, one is unable to decide whether to choose moderation or excess, light or obscurity, Apollo or Dionysus. Moments of such intensity make it difficult for anyone to ponder, or to distinguish between acts and their consequences.

The Impossible

In moments of intense ecstasy, everything condenses into one. It is impossible to distinguish between Apollo and Dionysus,[17] and all

---

16 According to the early fathers of the Church, the centre of the world, and hence its navel, is the intersection of the bars of the cross of Jesus.

17 According to Plutarch, Apollo and Dionysus took turns at Delphi, following a timetable of sorts. One or other would come to the fore depending on whether God would need to condense into a single entity, and hence into

that the individual experiences is an enormous vortex that removes it from the world of transparent moderation. The unfamiliar streams in through this crack, alienating one from everything, including oneself. This is when one discovers the navel of existence: something that is inherent in everything and yet transcends all there is; something that cannot be overtaken nor be left behind; something impossible that penetrates everything—that is NOT WHAT IT IS.

Ananke's Spindle

In the course of ancient festivals at Delphi, participants had often evoked the moment when Dionysus led his mother, the lightning-struck Semele, from Hades, the underworld, to Mount Olymp. This journey led through the navel of the Earth, from below upwards. The navel is also the seal of the underworld, of the beyond, to be precise, of which all we know is that it cannot be known. No one knows what it is like, except that it is Other, and the navel connects this Other with the known. Mythological descriptions in which the Earth is not a flat disk but an orb posit the navel as the point through which the axis supporting and piercing the globe emerges or vanishes.[18]

---

fire, or disperse and thus embody itself in the existent. When God turns into fire then

> the more enlightened, however, concealing from the masses the transformation into fire, call him Apollo because of his solitary state, and Phoebus because of his purity and stainlessness. And as for his turning into winds and water, earth and stars, and into the generations of plants and animals, and his adoption of such guises, they speak in a deceptive way of what he undergoes in his transformation as a tearing apart, as it were, and a dismemberment. They give him the names of Dionysus, Zagreus, Nyctelius, and Isodaetes (Plutarch, *On the E at Delphi* 9.5).

18 The tallest tree in Altai mythology, a fir tree that grows out of the navel of the Earth, has its crown reach up to the home of the sky god; Mesu, a holy

This invisible axis stuck into the navel of the Earth, akin to an eternally moving cosmic spindle, was interpreted in mythological descriptions as phallus, sexual intercourse and the axis of the world. The spindle has become one of the emblems associated with Heracles, to commemorate his time spent with queen Omphale, whom Heracles had to serve in female garments, despite retaining his gender. The queen had an intimate relationship with the navel of the Earth owing to the origin of her name (see Usener 1929), and she was a typical goddess of the underworld. The time Heracles spent with her can be interpreted as the hero's underworld journey. Omphale's power extends over the living and the dead in equal measure, and as such, she keeps watch over existence. The spindle she gave Heracles (whose 12 labours correspond to the Sun's orbit while crossing the zodiac) is an axis of the Earth: its ceaseless spinning turns the universe around.

This spindle, however, is not the exclusive property of Omphale. It also belongs to a more powerful mistress: Ananke, the goddess of need. According to Greek mythology, nothing would exist without her tying and weaving things together. There is a fastening that passes through Heaven and Earth, straight as a pillar of light, and holds the 'entire revolving vault' together, Plato writes in the *Republic* (616b–c). From the extremities of this fastening 'was stretched Ananke's spindle, through which all the orbits turned' and which

---

Sumerian tree, links the depth of the Earth with the sky; Jambutri-shring, the Tibetan tree of knowledge, is rooted in the kingdom of evil semi-gods but bears fruit in the kingdom of heavens; the saxon Irminsul buttress to everything and the pillar penetrating the universe, also vanishes into the navel of the Earth. The holy tree of Scandinavian mythology, Yggdrasil, onto which Odin was also sacrificially hung (crucifixion and resurrection in the mould of Dionysius and Christ), brings together space and time: it connects Heaven, Earth and Hell, is rooted in the past, lives in the present and stretches towards the future. Akin to other examples, this holy tree is also an axis of the world (axis mundi): it penetrates everything and the universe turns around it, as if it were a giant spindle.

'turned on the knees of Necessity' (*Republic* 616c–617b). This enormous spindle ensures that everything is interconnected and survives instead of falling back into chaos. In Ananke's lap there is an opening (mouth, vagina, navel wound), through which the conceivable joins the inconceivable so they can impregnate each other; and the spindle is the axis (phallus, umbilical cord, serpent, lightning), one end of which is rooted in existence and the other in the latter's absence. Epitomizing utmost necessity, the spindle holds everything captive, and consequently, is itself intangible. 'We are bound to one another by the inevitable law of our being,' Socrates contends in Plato's *Theaetetus* (160b): the very limitations of life make the human being realize that it has been put at the mercy of existence with no prospect for escape, and this was due to the whim of an unknown force. This whim, this obligatory fate (Ananke), from which one can only escape at the cost of one's life, keeps watch over it like a Fury; in fact, according to Orphism, the goddess of necessity and compulsion acts just like a Fury. Parmenides writes on Being (to eon):

> And remaining the same in the same place, it rests by itself and thus remains there fixed for powerful Necessity holds it in the bonds of a Limit, which constrains it round about, because it is decreed by divine law that Being shall not be without boundary. [. . . I]t is complete on every side, like the mass of a well-rounded sphere, equally balanced from its centre in every direction; for it is not bound to be at all either greater or less in this direction or that [. . .]. For, in all directions equal to itself, it reaches its limits uniformly (DK 28B8; Freeman 1983[1948] trans.).

Yet if there is and there will be Nothing in addition to the already existent, then is it conceivable for a boundary to surround it? Could Something that is beyond these boundaries, and which, strictly speaking, 'is not', still belong to the realm of the existent? And if it is only Ananke who is to be found beyond these boundaries, she who holds existence as such in her hand, could it not be that existence is permeated by Ananke who posits absence as the very 'foundation' of unfounded Being? Whenever one becomes aware of this (in moments of divine experience, inner lightning or finding the centre), the universe condenses into Ananke; and one is taken over by the desire to flee from its power, to step outside existence. Yet it is also in such moments that one realizes the futility of such attempts. Ananke is to be found in the individual too; by virtue of finding oneself surrendered to Being, one is also surrendered to one's own self.

The Magic of Now

It is difficult to give an account of the moment when the individual believes that it has found the centre. This is not due to transience or evanescence; on the contrary, one has never experienced oneself so collected, so grave and so peremptory. This moment is difficult to pin down because it is so grave: it is Being itself that is weighing one down. In such moments, Being becomes accessible, due to the fact that everything is suddenly bare, freed from the veil of the existent, the 'is'. In such moments, it becomes apparent that the existence of mankind is due to something that cannot be known, can never crystallize into something tangible and is impossible to speak of: it cannot even be called 'that'. Hence it emerges that the secret purpose of life is that Being can contradict itself through mankind—as the sole living entity in possession of reason and discretion yet subject to Being. As Peter Sloterdijk put it: 'In the meditations of genuine thinkers, but potentially in all human consciousness, it is the universe itself that is opening its eyes' (1993: 343). In such situations, the universe manifests itself through the individual, which appears as a giant wound on the body of Being that can only heal through the medium of death. As if it glanced into the world of the existent through a lightning-created crack in the sky, and found its mirror image, its transitory self—a self-portrait that in moments of intensity attempts to locate the centre of existence, the navel, yet the latter keeps refusing, mirage-like, to be pinned down.

The Measure

As Greek mythology perceptively illustrates, at the centre, or, to put it differently, at the navel of the Earth, one partakes of 'divine experience'. There is a particular attribute for Zeus: Panomphaios— All-Navel.[19] Regarding Zeus, Empedocles writes that 'there do not start two branches from his back; (he has) no feet, no swift knees, no organs of reproduction' (DK 31B29; Freeman 1983[1948] trans.), and has but one 'body part': the navel. Zeus is a giant navel. According to this, reaching the navel of the Earth and uniting with the centre of the universe is the equivalent of being initiated into the mysteries of the chief god, the one entirely Other.

The navel is the beginning and end of all that there is, the foundation and origin of things, and the measure of Being. Pythagoras—whose name can also mean the one who explains the Pythian (Delcourte 1955: 236)—observes in relation to the measure at the foundation of the universe: 'What is the Oracle of Delphi?— Tetractys, wherein is the harmony in which Sirens are' (DK 58C4). The tetractys, the sum of the first four numbers (1+2+3+4), represented the perfect number to Pythagoreans (10). They held the belief that it 'is the source of nature whose cause is eternal' (DK 58B15), and according to this, the navel is the measure of all measures: it is at the foundation of all measure and is thus immeasurable. This excess perpetuates be-ing beings, and encloses them within the hoops of measure. Measure could not exist without excess, and this becomes apparent in moments of so-called divine

---

19 Philolaus likened the centre of the orb, of the universe, that is, not only to the pit of all-combusting eternal fire but also to the house of Zeus (DK 44A16).

experience, of inner lightning, and discovery of the centre. This proliferates in everything and confronts the individual with all that transcends it. Without this, one could not exist.

The navel is a memento of birth; yet it would seem that, through the folds and creases, the impossible would also attempt to squeeze through, and thus make its presence known.

The Song of the Sirens

It is revealing that Pythagoras makes mention of the sirens. The fact that they also live in the navel of the universe means that, upon return, the individual comes across the centre as well as the sensation of homelessness. The sirens are Ananke's most loyal servants. According to mythological descriptions, the spindle of the goddess of compulsion is engaged with the turning around of seven disks; and thus in total there are eight circling orbits, including the spindle. On each of these 'a Siren stood, borne around in its revolution and uttering one sound, one note, and from all the eight there was the concord of a single harmony' (Plato, *Republic* 617b). The song of the sirens, the harmony of the spheres (the music of the planets) is irresistible, as the impossible is captured in their singing that is inaudible to human ear and that emanates from everything, permeating the individual too. This music can only be heard if one ventures beyond the universe and, as if breaking out of existence, contemplates it from afar—the position of eternal exclusion.

Yet is it death that hypnotizes the individual under the guise of the sirens? 'They sit in a meadow, and about them is a great heap of bones of mouldering men, and round the bones the skin is shrivelling,' Circe warns Ulysses (Homer, *Odyssey* 12.43–6). At times, the sirens appear as servants of Persephone, goddess of the underworld; in such cases, their song is a lament whereby it is existence that mourns itself. Whoever ends up hearing this song—be it in the howling of the wind, the breaking of the waves, the swishing of branches, the squealing of animals, the crashing of stones, in crying or growling, in laughter or sighing, in unfamiliar vibrations, the echo, the blood streaming in the arteries, the sound of tensed muscles, the beating of the heart, and even in silence itself—has already fallen victim to their charms. That person is lost to the navel of the Earth, joining in unawares and looking forward to being finally exposed to the prophecy of Being.

CHAPTER 4

THE LIMIT AND THE LIMITLESS

Caspar David Friedrich, *Evening* (1824)

Every moment is unique and special; it is not a mere continuation of other moments but also a new beginning. Creation starts anew in each and every instance, most spectacularly through origin and decay. The limitless does not signify the infinite beyond the limit, but that continuous and explosive vortex that makes every moment exceptional, disturbing and unparalleled, which prevents reconciliation and the halting of time so fervently desired by Faust. When crossing borders, one feels as if stepping out of time, and this is so because one suddenly becomes captive to the moment and is dazzled by the limitless beginning. While experiencing the beginning of the universe, one also realizes that this much-desired fulfilment is none other than living through the despondency of fulfilment.

Thus, it comes to light that, by obeying an inner yet simultaneously alien sound, one had been in pursuit of something that one should have in fact fled from: the experience of a singular life, and the dazzling pleasure of unrepeatability.

God isn't humanity's limit-point, though humanity's
limit-point is divine. Or put it this way—humanity is
divine when experiencing limits.

Georges Bataille (1988: 105)

Ixion's Wheel

No community could survive without the demarcation and obser-
vation of limits and boundaries. Religions that hold communities
together, and, above all, the ideologies emerging therefrom, however, tend to base their power on ignoring the fact that limits and
boundaries originate in something that is limitless and beyond moderation. Yet in each and every mythology, there are heroes who tres-
pass boundaries and lose all sense of moderation. It is revealing that
crossing boundaries is associated with terrible sin, and—especially
in Europe—with evil. Those who transgress the boundaries set out
by God are the harbingers of either chaos or Satan.

Trespassing boundaries, however, is not necessarily a sign of
evil; and wanting to transgress the world of moderation is not an
indication of hubris. Wanting to cross boundaries is rooted in a
sense of dissatisfaction that could be called cosmic, and cannot be
interpreted in a psychological manner. So why is this alarming then?
It is alarming because the individual can only free itself from the
burden of constraints and boundaries if assuming a new burden:
that of the boundless and the limitless. One discovers oneself in the
unknown, in the relatively perfect Other, but also in the impossible,
which prevents holding on to anything with confidence.

Ixion, like Sisyphus, Tantalus or Prometheus, is a well-known
icon of insatiability and excess. Akin to the others, he hails from

times immemorial; and his punishment represents the curtailment
of boundless passion by Zeus' orderly and moderate world. The
ancient king of Thessaly committed sin over sin; first he enticed his
father-in-law into a fiery trap, thus committing the first act of
familicide. Neither the humans nor the gods were prepared to
absolve him of his sin; yet Zeus took pity on this outlaw and not
only absolved him but also invited him to join the table of the gods,
thus immortalizing him. This incomer, however, abused Zeus' wel-
come. Lustful of the latter's wife, Hera, he fell into 'frantic' love with
her (Pindar, *Odes* 2.26), kissing her glass, sobbing at her feet and
begging for her favours. Zeus then fashioned a cloud to look like
Hera, and sent this copy to Ixion who was lying restless in bed. The
formerly mortal immortal was deceived by this likeness: he invited
the cloud into his bed, which led to the birth of the solitary and
fierce Centaur, the future father of the centaurs. Following this,
Zeus dispensed a never-ending punishment to Ixion: he had him
tied onto a burning wheel and sent him into space, with the aim to
make him spin around and chart an eternal path as either comet
or planet.[1]

The moral of the story seems obvious. As Pindar contends, 'A
man must always measure all things according to his own place',
or else, Man falls victim to hubris and 'extreme delusion' (*Odes*
2.34–5, 29). This perspective situates Zeus' order-centric world as
standard, despite not making direct reference to it; yet there are
several other revealing details in Ixion's story. One of these is the
forgiveness of familicide. This outcast sinner, having lost his reason,
was only pitied by Zeus, and as a result ended up condemned even
by the Furies. It is possible that Ixion's horrible deed conjured up
Zeus' own past, times when he himself—as the fortunate survivor
of serial familicides—would have butchered his opponents in a

---

1 According to another view, this Christ-like crucifixion of Ixion was in fact
aimed at restraining an earlier savage Sun God (Kerényi 1977: 108).

similarly excessive and possessed manner. Another detail is the fashioning of the Hera-cloud, through which Zeus apparently wanted to put his guest to the test. Though, being an omniscient God, could he not have foreseen what was taking place in Ixion's mind? Moreover—as an expert of transfiguration himself—could he not suspect that when Ixion has intercourse with the cloud, the man actually imagines Hera in his arms? Or else what could bring about his carnal pleasure? In fact, the sole aim of the ruse was to prevent Hera having intercourse with Ixion. Yet Zeus appears as a secret accomplice to the latter, and Lucian goes as far as to claim that the God had actually taken the mortal's side, and, rather than share Hera's indignant anger, tried to defend Ixion:

> Well, we have no one but ourselves to blame for it: we make too much of these mortals, admitting them to our table like this. When they drink of our nectar, and behold the beauties of Heaven (so different from those of Earth!), 'tis no wonder if they fall in love, and form ambitious schemes! Yes, Love is all-powerful; and not with mortals only: we Gods have sometimes fallen beneath his sway (Lucian, *Dialogues of the Gods* 9.6).

It is likely that Ixion reminded Zeus of the early days governed by excess, when he himself had to torment and coerce the universe in order to shape it into an orderly cosmos. Of all the gods, it is Zeus who should have known best that moderation is surrounded by excess. As a chief God, he recalled that the limitless is latent in all boundaries and limits, and also that the cosmos may well have emerged from chaos but chaos itself has not ceased to exist (see Reinhardt 1977: 174). Thus, Zeus must have recognized his own darker self in the mortal. The sense of enormity resurgent in Ixion and threatening the orderly world is not lurking somewhere outside or afar but is part and parcel of this very world. Ixion's punishment also suggests that in order to maintain order, some people have to be bound to a spoked wheel, or, rather, be used as a deterrent to put others off. It is only by means of such brutal interventions that the universe can be made to fit the mould of boundaries.[2]

Consequently, setting existence in order—in other words, the transformation of chaos into cosmos—might be the utmost imaginable punishment, might it not?

In the Shackles of the Limit

Zeus exiles those who transgress boundaries. Ixion is first sent to infinite space and then to the underworld, from where there is no return to the world of moderation. Thus, he has become one of the most fearsome figures in Greek mythology—as if fear had been embodied in him. And this is why the world of moderation needs safeguarding: in the wake of the limitless, excess becomes a threat without paying heed to anything.[3] Zeus entrusted the three Horae

---

2 People are usually crucified onto spoked wheels. For Plato the shape of the cross (X) is the first manifestation of the world's soul, and a precondition of the emerging globe-shaped universe (*Timaeus* 36b–c). Life engendered therefrom also follows the compulsion of cyclicality; and Aristotle rightly compared the compulsion for life to the wheel onto which people were bound to be tortured, and likened regular and eternal movement to a sense of unity—but also to Ixion's fate (*On the Heavens* 284a–b).

3 Nietzsche wrote on Zeus' world:

> As opposed to the toppled rule of the titans, Zeus' newly created world of gods bowed to the measure of beauty: the boundary within which Greeks had to be confined was the appearance of beauty. The innermost purpose of a culture fixated on appearance and moderation can only be the concealment of truth: both tireless truth-seekers and all-powerful titans receiving the same warning of 'méden agan' (1980a: 593).

Significantly, what Nietzsche calls truth becomes obvious in the ecstatic screams of the Festival of Dionysus, 'in which nature's whole excess of lust, suffering and recognition manifests itself. Everything that had thereto served as boundary and measure, appeared now as treacherous illusion: and "excess" revealed itself as truth' (ibid.: 593–4).

to keep watch over Olymp; it is their duty 'either to open the dense cloud [. . .], or to close it' (Homer, *Iliad* 5.75). Very little is known of their origin and lives: the guardians of moderation are unknown. All three embody order, yet they are soaring and unsurpassed. Being in charge of the cycle of seasons and the rhythm of life more generally, they are able to transcend this rhythm and cyclicality. Not even their names can be known with any certainty. According to Plato, their names mean 'limit' (*Cratylus* 410d), and according to Hesiod, Legal Order (Eunomia), Peace (Eirene) and Rightful Reward (Dike) (*Theogony* 901–02).

The name Dike draws attention yet again to compulsion as inseparable from existence. Plato contends in this regard:

O men, that God who, as old tradition tells, holdeth the beginning, the end, and the center of all things that exist, completeth his circuit by nature's ordinance in straight, unswerving course. With him followeth Justice, as avenger of them that fall short of the divine law; and she, again, is followed by every man who would fain be happy, cleaving to her with lowly and orderly behavior; but whoso is uplifted by vainglory, or prideth himself on his riches or his honors or his comeliness of body, and through this pride joined to youth and folly, is inflamed in soul with insolence, dreaming that he has no need of ruler or guide, but rather is competent himself to guide others such an one is abandoned and left behind by the God, and when left behind he taketh to him others of like nature, and by his mad prancings throweth all into confusion: to many, indeed, he seemeth to be some great one, but after no long time he payeth the penalty, not unmerited, to Justice, when he bringeth to total ruin himself, his house, and his coun- try. [. . .] 'like is dear to like' when it is moderate, whereas immoderate things are dear neither to one another nor to things moderate. In our eyes God will be 'the measure of all things' in the highest degree—a degree much higher than is any 'man' they talk of (*Laws* 715e–716d).

In this view, the limit is guarded by those who are themselves limitless; and whoever, in their 'conceit', aspires to limitlessness is after all on a quest for freedom that is the attribute of gods alone. A fragment credited to Philolaus argues: 'gods look after us; we are one of the possessions of the gods' (DK 44B15; Freeman 1983[1948] trans.); but it is possible for the original text to have read as follows: 'we are in a sort of watch-tower which we must not desert [. . .] we are one of the possessions of the gods' (ibid). Man is God's prisoner; and Parmenides labels the 'often punishing' Dike a *prison guard* (DK 28B1). 'Justice (Dike) has never released (Being) in its fetters and set it free either to come into being or to perish, but hold it fast' (ibid.). Dike carries out the same task as Ananke, the Goddess of necessity, who also restrains existence and who has fettered the sky and 'constrained it to hold the limits of the stars' (ibid.). It is no coincidence that the Mithras-mysteries would summon Dike alongside Ananke (Schreckenberg 1964: 161), as everything that there is finds itself in their shackles; even the gods themselves are at their mercy.

The Horae keep watch over limits and moderation, without which existence would be inconceivable. The Horae are situated beyond limits and moderation, as it is limitlessness and excess that manifest through them. Although they take care of existence, they are inscrutable, and it is difficult to include them into the realm of the existent.

Overwhelming Absence

'We are bound to one another by the inevitable law of our being,' Plato writes in *Theateteus* (160b), using the term *hé ananké*. The human being, by virtue of its sheer existence, is at the mercy of moderation, the limit and the world of order. As long as existence instils confidence, all this comes across as natural and self-evident. A single disruptive moment is sufficient, however, to experience the fact that one is the least in control over the sole thing that is the utmost proof of existence: one's life. One has not requested life from anyone yet has ended up as its recipient, and similarly has no say in its loss. In moments of disruption, it becomes apparent that moderation is a prison, and, as its tenant, one is the prisoner of those who surpass existence altogether: Dike and Ananke; in other words, limitlessness and excess. Thus, one has to become limitless and immoderate in order to assess the totality of one's own existence; and paradoxically, captivity ends up bearable as a result of the unbearable. One finds oneself in the limitless having left behind the boundaries of the limit; and despite everything being devoid of its weight, one does not feel weightless at all. In spite of the all-embracing negation, one's being is permeated by an infinite 'yes', through which the limitless manifests itself. The very instances of border crossing shed light on the fact that one owes one's life to the all-surpassing intangible, and not to limits and moderation. In such uber-moments, one is just as unsurpassed and limitless as any supposed god, and is invigorated by conflict and paradox—termed war by Heraclitus and all-pervasive hell by Jakob Böhme. Even though by crossing borders one is overtaken by the passion of death, it is not death that one upholds but the inconceivable and the unbearable, both of which supersede life and death alike: in other words, existence fuelled by negation itself.

The Depth of Logos

'You could not in your going find the ends of the soul, though you travelled the whole way: so deep is its Law (Logos)', observes Heraclitus (DK 22B45, Freeman 1983[1948] trans.). The soul, due to the logos therein, is inscrutable. The soul is impenetrable, though not owing to its immeasurable size or depth but because of its limitlessness: as limited limitlessness, it is simultaneously within and beside itself. 'The soul has its own Law (Logos), which increases itself (i.e. grows according to its needs),' Heraclitus notes in another fragment (DK 22B115, Freeman 1983[1948] trans.). Logos is the 'property' of the soul, and resides within its boundaries; yet this same logos is so broad and limitless that, like the infinite, it can surround the soul from the outside. Due to a perpetual and magical shift of perspective, the soul is inaccessible: sometimes the soul is to be found in logos, other times the logos in the soul, depending on which of them is at risk of being confined by limits. When approaching the soul, logos becomes incomprehensible, without which the soul cannot be known either; approaching logos, however, the soul appears infinitely distant, and without the latter, there is no possibility of knowledge. 'The Law (Logos): though men associate with it most closely, yet they are separated from it, and those things which they encounter daily seem to them strange,' Heraclitus observes (DK 22B72, Freeman 1983[1948] trans.). The soul is unable to grab logos because it is already inherent therein; and what is yet to be determined turns out to be identical with the determinate.

Since the soul is the 'property' of the self, when it obeys logos it also experiences the limitless. According to logos, everything is one, Heraclitus claims (DK 22B50); and by crossing boundaries one does not fall apart but, on the contrary, pulls oneself together, and one's diverse and incompatible desires and aims find themselves united in a single goal. On the one hand, the individual leaves the city behind and turns its back on it; on the other, it would appear that the world is starting to look like a world at this very point. Sloterdijk alerts us to look for the origins of 'psychology' in 'acosmology', and connects this to Plato: 'The decisive information about the soul's actual nature has been obtainable ever since by means of a *via negativa*, through the thinking away of the world and through deletion of sensory world traces. Soul is Being, except for participation in an inhibiting cosmos' (1993: 174–5). The Heraclitian relationship between soul and logos cautions us that there is a—to this day marginalized—alternative strand in European culture in which the soul does not find itself up against the world but, on the contrary, by means of 'incorporation'. A precondition of this is to find a common ground between the soul and the world, which is the logos. Logos 'opens up' the soul to the temporal world while preventing the reduction of the 'world' to lifeless matter. In moments of being touched by logos (which we could also call divine experience), differences between countless alternative options suddenly become irrelevant, and the awareness of unity, the perception of the shared quality of be-ing beings, gains precedence. This is when the 'path' to Being opens up, also likened by Heraclitus to the paths leading towards the limits of the soul.

Crossing borders signifies, in fact, starting out into the unknown. Everything that there is can be classed as limited and finite; but by sheer virtue of this, it also benefits from limitless Being. The 'is' is pregnant with the 'is not', and existence with non-existence: they grind and wear each other out, taking care meanwhile of the origin and decay of the existent. Akin to a giant vortex, they are in the service of Being, which, as a limitless entity, absorbs and incorporates everything. For this reason, the Pythagoreans also called Unity Chaos, the etymology of which links back to the verb 'yawn'. When crossing borders, the individual cannot be sure if one is engaged in the act of taking another step or if there is something else out there that actually engulfs one.

The Limitlessness of the Beginning

By crossing borders, one comes closer to one's own self, and thus it appears as if the beginning and ultimate goal of everything also become clearer. Beginning is limitless by definition; otherwise something else would be about to begin right beyond a previous beginning. Limitlessness signifies not only greatness but force too; hence the beginning by definition surpasses what is to follow in its wake. The limitless, in fact, is beginning and master of the universe at once, and the Greek term *arkhé* means both beginning and master.

What, in fact, is beginning? Pre-Socratic philosophers explained everything with reference to the elements: Anaximenes to air, Heraclitus to fire, Thales to water. The original meaning of the word nature (*physis*), however, demonstrates that we are not dealing with a strictly physical notion of the elements. Pre-Socratics associated nature with the all-encompassing Being (see Heidegger 1978: 258), which surpasses nature interpreted in a physical sense. Xenophanes' book on nature (*Peri Physeos*) addresses, above all, the question of inconceivable existence and the invisible God. Anaximenes qualifies air as divine, in order to suggest the infinite quality inherent in the beginning (DK 13A10). When Thales mentions water, he draws attention, in fact, to the unity of Being, considered to be divine. By naming a single element, he tried to suggest—quoting an early work of Nietzsche—'the harmony of the world', and, despite referring to water, he did not restrict his focus to this element; his goal was to elaborate on something that, in Nietzsche's words, 'could only be conveyed by way of gestures and music' (1980b: 817; 1980c: 110). According to Heraclitus, the most typical characteristic of nature is not measurability, graspability or perceptibility, but truth and wisdom; and by virtue of its ubiquity, nature also withdraws itself from everything as an incomprehensible Unity.[4] The ur-element, the beginning of the universe is something that is visible and accessible;

---

4 '[Moderation is the greatest virtue], and wisdom is to speak the truth and to act according to nature, paying heed (*thereto*)' (DK 22B112, Freeman 1983[1948] trans.).

in other words, it surpasses the nature that can be enclosed into boundaries like Being surpasses existence:[5] and it takes care of the formation of limits by virtue of its very limitlessness.

The indisputable simplicity of terms referring to this ur-element is rooted in a paradoxical experience: that of the oneness of Being. An often-debated claim by Anaximandros makes this most obvious, since he names limitlessness itself as an ur-element: 'The Non-Limited (*apeiron*) is the original material (*arkhé*) of existing things' (DK 12B1, Freeman 1983[1948] trans.). By introducing the term *apeiron*, the kind of misapprehension possible in the case of water, fire or air is excluded: this 'element', since it is all-comprising, cannot be comprehended by means of calculation, measurement or experiment (DK 12B9).[6] *Apeiron* means limitless and infinite, excluding factuality by definition. As Károly Kerényi put it: Anaximandros 'chose as ur-element the unlimited richness of potential, something without a material form and viewed from a negative point of view, akin to the *kat' exokhén* "limitless" and the naturally undefinable *apeiron*' (1983: 65). The word is etymologically rooted in the term *peras* (meaning border), fitted with a privative affix. The fact that the ultimate border is something that cannot be enclosed, in other words, the ultimate determinate cannot be determined, is indicated by the root *per-*, *peri-* which gives away that it is connected to transcendence rather than enclosure. The border is part of what it borders on, yet it also communicates with what is beyond; it simultaneously

---

5 Plato notes the following in *Theaetetus*: 'the primary elements of which we and all else are composed admit of no rational explanation; for each alone by itself can only be named, and no qualification can be added, neither that it is nor that it is not, for that would at once be adding to it existence or non-existence, whereas we must add nothing to it, if we are to speak of that itself alone' (201e–202a).

6 This view does not clash with the later analysis put forward by Hippolytus, according to whom *apeiron* is a physical phenomenon (*physis*—see DK 12B10), as long as we rely on the original, comprehensive meaning of *physis*.

divides and connects (the English word *ferry* can be traced back to the root *per-*). The border exists (since it separates and connects), and does not exist (since one cannot actually stand on the border: one is either here or there). The border connotes cross-border traffic. It does not only signify the closure of something but also its inspection, and hence cognition (the Greek term *empiria* and the Latin *experientia* derive from *per-*). Borders determine; as Aristotle explains, the border is both the very edge of something and its shape, aim, essence, 'why' and 'how'—since these aspects represent the boundaries of cognition and, by extension, of things too (*Metaphysics* 5.1022).

Pantos panta peronta ('one should go through all the things'—Freeman 1983[1948] trans.), Parmenides contended (DK 28B1): in the universe everything permeates everything (*peiran* means attacking or charging something; *peirates* means pirate). Limits and boundaries are ubiquitous (beings are distinguished from one another by virtue of delimitation) yet also at the vanishing point: they can be infinitely 'pushed' further or farther. The universe is limitless because there is Nothing beyond it and it has no borders: the universe is its own utmost limit; in other words, its only 'border' is the limitless, which can crop up in everything. The universe transcends everything; therefore, it is beginning itself. This ensures that communication between all that is confined and the infinite takes place (irrespective of what is confined into boundaries, the boundless universe is to be found beyond), and, moreover, that the former charges itself by means of the latter.

Apeiron is not the infinite beyond boundaries but a continuous explosive vortex that transforms every moment into something exceptional and disruptive. Thus, *apeiron* draws attention to the eternal danger inherent in the fraud of limited existence. Each moment is unique and special, not merely as a continuation of others but also as a fresh beginning. For this reason, when crossing borders, Man experiences the dazzle of limitless beginning, and

partakes of the curious and vortex-like experience of life's uniqueness and unrepeatability.

The Inexhaustible

Commitment to moderation and respect for limits is a precondition
of human communities. Crossing borders is 'hostile to community'
from all points of view. The tragic experience cannot be rounded
into any system, yet human coexistence cannot be imagined in the
absence of some kind of system. Obviously, the latter would not
need to be despotic by definition; it becomes despotic if a community or society is not prepared to acknowledge that its indispensable
organization is after all just as pointless as life itself, and that, akin
to any plant, is condemned to wilting and decay. As several ancient
or non-European cultures demonstrate, if a community does not
want to delimit itself from the cosmos (and does not perceive it as
an object of 'research' or subjugation), but, rather, wishes to fit into
its overarching system, then it is also capable of integrating the subversive and tragic experience of border crossing. Let us consider
sacrifice, prodigality, worshipping conflicting sacraments, attitudes
to death, or the indispensable role of tragedy as a form of audience
management in various cultures in this sense. On the other hand,
if a community fails to do this, then it has no choice but to stigma-
tize border crossing as sin, and label it as the mark of bigotry.

If existence is reduced to something tangible, comprehensible,
thinkable, imaginable or definable, then there is no such thing as
the limitless. In such cases, only what has not yet been determined
can be considered limitless. Could being enclosed and determined,
however, be classed as the ultimate claim one could posit in relation
to existence? Provided there is indeed Nothing beyond the ultimate
frontier, could this Nothing really refrain from nestling, parasite-
like, into existence and thus planting the seeds of its own lack? The
limitless, owing to the fact that 'one should go through all the

things', is not the infinite quality of depth, height, greatness, weight or distance, but, rather, of the inexhaustible. In moments of divine experience, lightning or approaching the centre, it is this that conveys to everything that there is a strange and blinding radiance. It is by way of the limitless that all that invigorates limit-bound be-ing beings manifests itself; and if thought is incapable to encompass the infinite, then this is not a sign of the latter's imperfection, as Aristotle claims,[7] but of the fact that the thinkable has actually been crystallized from the unthinkable.

Once More on Divine Experience

The limitless is to be found not beyond but within limits. It even offers the possibility for the individual to attempt transgressing boundaries. Not owing to hubris, curiosity, spirit of adventure, but in order to come closer to the thing that it owes its existence to. By

---

7 Aristotle considers the infinite as a form of negativity, as something onto which more things can be added, and, as a result, it is never complete or whole. Consequently, Aristotle shares the pre-Socratic view—according to which, *apeiron*, the limitless, comprises everything and there is nothing else in addition to it—untenable. In his view, the infinite is the very opposite of this: something beyond which there is always something else. Yet, something onto which more can be added cannot be whole; because

> what has nothing outside it is complete and whole. For thus we define the whole that from which nothing is wanting, as a whole man or a whole box. What is true of each particular is true of the whole as such—the whole is that of which nothing is outside. On the other hand that from which something is absent and outside, however small that may be, is not all. 'Whole' and 'complete' are either quite identical or closely akin. Nothing is complete (*teleion*) which has no end (*telos*); and the end is a limit (Aristotle, *Physics* 3.6; 2006: 128–9).

This interpretation of the limitless is radically different from that of the pre-Socratics. While pre-Socratics viewed the infinite as a force ensuring the unity of the universe, Aristotle saw the universe as the sum of graspable things, the overall number of which is finite. This definition of the universe, however, refers—in modern parlance—to a universe devoid of magic.

crossing the border, it becomes apparent that this was not a voluntary act, and one in fact obeyed a calling that only became audible in the very moment of crossing. In order to be able to talk about this calling at a later point, one brings up 'God'. There is a single superhuman being susceptible to the magical ability of moving into anyone with the aim of alienating this individual from its own self. The infinite has always been considered divine, as Thales, the first Greek sage observes: 'the divine is that which has neither beginning nor end' (DK 11A1). This is the reason why one connotes border crossing with divine experience: should God choose to appear, no border or limit could keep him out. In his discussion of Abraham's divine vision, first-century scholar Philo went as far as drawing on linguistics in order to suggest the limitless quality of this experience: he traces the attribute 'Hebrew' associated with Abraham's name (1 Moses 14:13) to the root '*br*, which is connected to departure and the idea of permeation. Hence, Philo translates 'Hebrew' as *perates* (Philo, *On the Migration of Abraham* 20), the literal meaning of which is something that permeates (*peirates* = pirate).[8] Abraham is the first Hebrew, the first seer—the first border crosser.

The God that appears in front of the border crosser, however, does not bring peace. Abraham was overtaken by a 'terrifying kind of darkness' when God surprised him at dusk (1 Moses 15:12). By means of divine experience, it was the limitless that entered his life— something that casts the individual out of its self. The limitless is concealed not in the 'Nothing' beyond existence but in the Nothing inherent in existence; it is not the God beyond Being who would govern everything from the outside, as imagined by the Gnostics, but a vortex that continually keeps existence twisting and turning.

---

8 The '*br*- root, present in all Semitic languages, is at the origin of terms such as 'across' ('over') (Genesis 32:23; 1 Samuel 13:23), 'transgress the king's command' (Esther 3:3), being 'over' (Genesis 50:4, 2 Samuel 11:27), figuratively 'pass away' (Job 34:20), 'the Lord passed by' (1 Kings 19:11), God's punishing 'passing over' (Exodus 12:12–3) (see Jenni and Westermann 1976: 200–02).

Should one be able to pull oneself out of this paradox, the outcome would not be tranquillity but non-Being. The latter, however, has no means to manifest itself, and hence can no longer be qualified as limitless.

The Impossible

Where does the transgression of boundaries lead to? Presumably to the limitless. But can the excessive be still considered in terms of limitlessness? Could this in fact be a paradox? Does not the individual's crossing over cast aside everything, including all appellations? Is not there a glimmer of the IMPOSSIBLE in all that awaits the individual? Is not the 'limitless' just an awkward linguistic code for something that cannot even be called limitless? After all, could the pronoun 'that' be utilized at all in the dawning presence of the entity that both makes the use of language possible and sets its boundaries? Is this not the manifestation of something that cannot even be called 'that', only THAT, THAT IS NOT THAT? And last but not least, having just surmised this, should not speech be silenced altogether?

CHAPTER 5

YAWNING CHAOS

Portrait of the Four Tetrarchs, Venice

Chaos tends to overcome the individual in moments fraught with internal contradiction: when one begins to simultaneously feel like a timeless and peculiar being that experiences life as a miracle, and a time-bound mortal who is only able to enjoy this miracle while also experiencing their own passing. In such moments, unconcealed being becomes truly experiential: one experiences oneself as exceptional, surpassing all others, in whom all existence is condensed, and yet also finds oneself at the mercy of the beginning and the whims of existence, someone whose life is nothing but embodied chance. Thus, *the universe* mirrors the *uniqueness* of life; and the *completeness* of the whole is indistinguishable from the *fragmentation* inherent in uniqueness. The fraction is whole, because it is unique, exceptional, unmistakable and irreplaceable—since its life is unrepeatable, too. And yet, it is but a part, a fragment, a chip—akin to a sharp shard of glass that cannot be taken in hand, but in which the entire existence glares back, including the shard itself that keeps on reflecting its own self, over and over again, in ways impossible to trace or follow.

*That there was a Deluge once, seemes not to me so
great a Miracle, as that there is not one alwayes.*

Thomas Browne (1964a: 1.22)

The Throat

The following story is narrated in the Old Testament. On the twelfth
day of the tenth month in the tenth year, the Lord called the son of
man, priest Ezekiel, to set his face against the Pharaoh, king of
Egypt, and prophesy against him: 'Behold, I am against you,
Pharaoh king of Egypt, the great monster that lies in the midst of
his rivers, who has said, My river is my own, and I have made it for
myself' (Ezekiel 29:3). The crocodile turned out to be a 'staff of reed'
to the house of Israel; therefore, his perishment would lead to salvation. According to the anonymous author of a surprisingly daring
work of natural history compiled in the second century and entitled
Physiologus, the death of the crocodile would signify the victory of
Christ the Saviour over Satan.

Yet it is not only force that is needed in order to defeat the
crocodile. Cunning, too—to be precise, the cunning of the ichneumon, the pharaoh's rat (*Herpestes ichneumon*). According to the
Physiologus, whenever this rat comes across a crocodile, it 'besmears
himself with mud and covers his nostrils with his tail' until such
time that its enemy is dead (*Physiologus* 26). But how does it kill
them? Oppian, the author of a third-century poem on hunting,
describes the battle: in order to conceal itself, the ichneumon covers
its small body with mud and, squatting motionless in the vicinity
of the crocodile, waits until its enemy opens its jaws to yawn and
flash its awe-inspiring row of teeth. At the point when the crocodile
can no longer stretch its mouth any further, the ichneumon jumps

straight into its throat, descends into its stomach and starts gorging on its liver. The crocodile is in raging pain, and would want to fight in case there was anyone to fight with; it keeps running up and down in despair, until it finally passes away in agony. Then the ichneumon crawls out to light, revealing the glory of the natural world.

When describing the sleeping crocodile, Oppian uses a peculiar expression: he calls its wide-open mouth and cavernous throat *chaos eury*—wide throat (*Cynegetica* 3.414). Therefore, the ichneumon jumps into *a wide-open throat*, and hence into *chaos*. According to the author of *Physiologus*, Christ had to descend in order to annihilate Evil, while the pharaoh's rat has to penetrate chaos. The road to victory therefore leads through chaos; but, viewed from here, the wide throat is *death*, and viewed from there, the gate of *eternal life*. By annihilating the crocodile, the ichneumon overcomes chaos, so to speak. We could of course also see this as if chaos first swallowed and then spat out the pharaoh's rat: the origin of the word 'chaos' is the Indo-Germanic *ĝhēu-* connected to swallowing and yawning (the Greek *chaino* means to yawn) (Pokorny 1959: 419).

The *yawning throat* is an abyss that leads to darkness—a darkness that conceals organs and entrails, darkens the veins, intestines, flesh and blood, fills the chambers of the heart and the alveoles of the lungs, and permeates bones, tissues and the brain. The organs that ensure the necessaries of life are concealed in the dark, and the funnel-like throat reaches down to this very darkness. Chaos is rooted in this invisibility down below, yet it attempts to seep out through the wide-open mouth.

The ichneumon sits still on the banks of the Nile, waiting for the crocodile to yawn. Then it jumps into the wide-open throat. But could it really be as cunning as Oppian had thought? Does it really plot a plan, like Christ did against Evil? Could it not be that it was the crocodile that charmed it into stillness? We can imagine that when the crocodile opened its mouth wide, the freshly revealed chaos actually drew in an already paralysed being. If this supposition is correct, then the crocodile is the representative of an even mightier and more threatening force, that of chaos itself.

The Mouth of the Crocodile

The sheer sight of the crocodile is 'overwhelming', the Lord warns Job; 'his rows of scales are his pride, shut up tightly as with a seal', 'strength dwells in his neck, and sorrow dances before him' (Job 41:9, 15, 22). The figure of the crocodile has been shrouded in mystery since time immemorial. Owing to its hardly noticeable tiny tongue, the Egyptians perceived it as the embodiment of divine silence (Plutarch, Isis and Osiris 75), and venerated it with the piety reserved for the 'masters' of silence, such as Harpocrates or Pythagoras. They also drew the conclusion that the membrane covering its eye was an indication of divine capabilities: akin to God, the crocodile would also see everything without anyone being able to detect its glance. Analysing the structure of its body, they discovered a peculiar system: according to Aelianus, a natural scientist active at the turn of the second and third centuries, crocodiles have 60 teeth, 60 vertebrae and 60 tendons (On the Characteristics of Animals 10.211); they lay 60 eggs,[1] which hatch after 60 days; they live for 60 years and for 60 days each year they eat nothing, during which time they represent no harm. Plutarch argues that this is the reason why number 60 became the unit of measurement for studying celestial phenomena (Isis and Osiris 75). According to these thinkers, the crocodile's body charts the correlations of the universe, though for second-century author Achilles Tatius, crocodiles do not have 60 teeth but as many as there are days in the year: the Earth rotates around the Sun in 365 days to complete its crocodile-style journey (Achilles Tatius, The Adventures of Leucippe and Clitophon, 4.19). To turn this correlation even more mysterious, the Romans

---

1 There are views according to which the dog-like barking of cockerels and their laying of eggs leads to the hatching of crocodiles (Ipolyi 1854: 585).

also called the two-faced Janus, who, according to Pliny, had 365 fingers, Chaos—a name that alludes to the all-devouring 365-toothed crocodile: 'The ancients called me Chaos, for a being from of old am I' (Ovid, *Fasti* 1.103).

It is *chaos* that opens up in the crocodile's throat, yet the system manifest in its body is symbolic of the organization of the universe, and of *cosmos* itself, in the original sense of the word. This led to ambivalent reactions, and it was seen as sacred and evil at the same time. Herodotus notes that the Egyptians, especially in the area of Thebes and Lake Moiris, considered it sacred (*Histories* 2.69), and Aelianus contends that the inhabitants of Ombos believed that children grabbed and devoured by crocodiles were truly happy since they ended up as nourishment for gods and thus made it to the best possible place (*On the Characteristics of Animals* 10.21).[2]

On the other hand—advancing a medieval Christian iconographic tradition whereby the crocodile is symbolic of the devil, in addition to the dragon and the serpent[3]—the Egyptians (especially around Elephantis) saw it as a stand-in for harmful forces. On the whole, the ancient Egyptian crocodile-God, Sobek (Suchos), did have 'celestial' implications (he was likened to Ra, and by the Greeks, to Helios); however, he was an envoy of the dark and deep recesses of the Earth: his mother was Neith, Goddess of war and the dead, whose attribute is 'the path opener'. Neith is treading ahead of everyone, followed by her crocodile son, through whose

---

2 According to the Egyptian Book of the Dead, corpses become food for crocodiles (*The Book of the Dead* 1974: 42).

3 In France, in 1776 the devil appeared in the shape of a crocodile to Dutoit-Mambrini, notes Simonne Rihouet-Coroze in his preface to a work by Louis-Claude de Saint-Martin (one of Franz von Baader's favourite authors!). This politically inclined book, finalized in 1792 and published in 1798, also has a revealing title: *Le Crocodile ou la guerre du bien et du mal arrivée sous le règne de Louis XV. Poème epico-magique (en prose)* [*The Crocodile, or the War of Good and Evil under the Reign of Louis XV: A Magical Epic Poem in Prose*] (see Saint-Martin 1979: 19).

wide-open throat the unknown pours in, only to depart in the shape of organized cosmos.

The harmful and chaotic force of the crocodile is best high-lighted by the fact that it was also seen as an embodiment of Seth, known as Typhon in Greek. Typhon killed Osiris, the chief God who has tamed humans and helped organize human life; and he is the one who 'because of his ignorance and self-deception [. . .] tears to pieces and scatters to the winds the sacred writings' (Plutarch, *Isis and Osiris* 2),[4] and about whom legend has it that 'prompted by jealousy and hostility, he wrought terrible deeds and, by bringing utter confusion upon all things, filled the whole Earth, and the ocean as well, with ills' (ibid. 27). Plutarch observes that Osiris is the manifestation of everything that is regular, permanent, healthy and moderate; by contrast, Seth-Typhon 'is that part of the soul which is impressionable, impulsive, irrational and truculent, and of the bodily part the destructible, diseased and disorderly as evidenced by abnormal seasons and temperatures, and by obscu-rations of the sun and disappearances of the moon' (ibid. 49). Excess and disorder come to the fore through Seth-Typhon, and it has been said about him that he 'escaped Horus by turning into a crocodile' (ibid. 50).

Seth-Typhon embodies cosmos-threatening chaos. As a result, Seth was also seen as a giant who provoked storms and earth-quakes, and for this, the Sethian sect of the Gnostics held him in high esteem as 'an invincible God', 'the almighty', 'the creator of Gods'. Seth-Typhon, the God shape-shifting into a crocodile, draws us into the very vortex that also appears in the chaos at the bottom of the crocodile's throat. In this everything that is otherwise

---

4 On the island of La Gonave near Haiti, inhabitants continued to be fearful of a crocodile up until the 1920s. No one had dared to kill it, and it lived in a bottomless lake. 'The natives are afraid to let him be shot, and even sometimes provide food for him; he has been there from beyond the memory of man, and perhaps incarnates one of their *mystères*' (Seabrook 1929: 196).

separable, visible and comprehensible—in other words, is expressed
in moderation—due to exposure to the grinding of teeth equalling
the number of days in a year, becomes excessive, indistinguishable
and incomprehensible—that is, it becomes subject to chaos.

Chaos Is Beyond Order and Confusion

The chaos whirling in Typhon's throat grabs everything in its reach,
just like a typhoon. The God's very name hints at severe gales
(typhoon): the Indo-Germanic *dheu-*, *dhuə-* root is connected to
whirlpools and whirlabouts (Pokorny 1959: 261). (The Greek
typhos = whirlwind, *thymos* = passion, old Germanic *tobon* = to be
frantic, and the Anglo-Saxon *dofian* = to rage—all can be traced
back to this origin.) The whirlwind displaces everything, and makes
it impossible for anyone to decide while it lasts whether the world
is orderly or chaotic. It is this ultimate indecision that manifests
itself in chaos. Gale, whirlwind, all-engulfing throat: a vortex in
which everything that there is creates the impression of either
divine orderliness, or total confusion.

Chaos is beyond everything. And although it could not even
manifest itself if it did not don some kind of visible mask, such a
guise is always threatening—be it the mask of confusion, or, conversely, of order. They both give grounds for suspicion, as far as an
underlying and inscrutable force is concerned. This force can be
called neither order nor confusion, since the latter has meaning
only in relation to order. Chaos cannot be likened to anything that
is perceptible, that there is or that exists, because all these are mere
states which will soon give way to other, equally legitimate states.
Chaos ensures that things originate and decay, that they take turns,
follow and consume one another, and that they are able to exist at
all—to be precise, they are let loose into existence, coming from a
place where there is Nothing but which nevertheless appears as the
womb of the entire existence. Chaos makes it possible for anything

that there is to come into being. For this reason, chaos itself cannot be labelled as something that is, or something that is not; it backs out of everything despite Nothing being actually able to exist without it. Chaos is something that is not even identical with its own self; something that, instead of grounding everything as the 'ultimate foundation', is more likely to pull the ground from beneath everything like a 'groundless' and 'bottomless abyss'.[5]

Chaos cannot be likened to anything, and it cannot be discussed in terms of 'it is' or 'it is not': It is something that IS NOT WHAT IT IS. Hence, its meaning is unparalleled, too: it is impossible to prepare for or, indeed, avoid it. No wonder it offers primal experiences to Man. When the life-giving and unifying force that sets beings into motion, when the intangible and unbearable being is tamed and made tangible through sheer naming, in other words, when the IMPOSSIBLE protrudes, then one partakes of the experience of chaos.

The Allness of the One

Whenever one seeks explanations for the fissures that have the capacity to tilt and jumble up the previously well-balanced course of life, then chaos—this crocodile-like and all-engulfing ultimate foundation—tends to come to mind. Hesiod notes: 'Verily at the first Chaos came to be, but next wide-bosomed Earth, the ever-sure foundations of all, [. . .] and Eros (Love), fairest among the deathless gods [. . .]. From Chaos came forth Erebus and black Night; but of Night were born Aether and Day' (*Theogony* 116–24).

According to Babylonian cosmology, in the beginning there was only Chaos (Mummu), linked to the figure of Tiamat the

---

5 Anticipating medieval mystics, Saint Augustine names chaos 'shapeless matter', 'almost nothing', following which—turning to the concept of the abyss and vortex—he notes: 'of all things having form, nothing is nearer to the formless than the earth and the deep' (*Confessions* 12.19)

dragon (its name means sea), and Chaos' companion, Apsu, connoting depth, originary unity and fresh water. Their union led to the birth of several generations of Gods. Chaos is the first element in Phoenician cosmogony, too; he unites with Pneuma, the fertilizing wind, and their encounter brings about the emergence of desire. The three of them beget Mot (Mavet), who is closely linked to primeval water, and then Mavet gives birth to the egg that encloses the entire universe.[6]

In this view, chaos is the common foundation for an infinite number of be-ing beings, and embodies their oneness. Pythagoreans rightly named One as Chaos: without One there would be no numbers (there would be no basis for counting), yet One as such (according to the Greeks) is not part of the number sequence since, as a beginning of sorts, it precedes it. According to the Pythagoreans, One is both an odd and an even number, is both limited and limitless, empty and charged (Aristotle, *Physics* 4.6.233b). It has no limits, since otherwise it would be limited; it cannot be considered limitless either, by virtue of its uniqueness and exclusiveness. It cannot be perceived as existent, because—as the foundation to all that is existent—it is excluded from existence; yet it cannot be seen as non-existent either, because—in the absence of existence—it could not manifest itself either. One experiences chaos when falling victim to these contradictions: in the experience of All-Is-One, the limitless feeling of life is paired with the feeling of life's oppressive Nothingness. Thus, this allness ends up mirroring the uniqueness of life; and the wholeness of the all is undistinguishable from the fragmentation inherent in

---

6 A similar idea is described in the New Testament, except for the fact that the role of Chaos is taken over by the Lord (Jahve) or God (Elohim); but there are references to both spirit and water: 'In the beginning God created the heavens and the earth. The earth was without form, and void [meaning disorderly, in Hebrew: *tóhu-va-bóhu*]; and darkness was on the face of the deep. And the Spirit of God was hovering over the face of the waters' (Genesis 1:1–2).

uniqueness. The fraction is whole, because it is unique, exceptional, unmistakable and irreplaceable—since everything is but a fragment. And yet, it is only a fragment, a chip that cannot be integrated into anything, and hence only exists for its own sake—akin to a shard of glass, in which, as if in a magic mirror, the entire existence glares back, including the shard itself which keeps on reflecting its own self, over and over again.

The Beginning of the Beginning

Mythological explanations posit Chaos as the beginning of the universe, yet such cosmologies tend to be rather vague. 'At first Chaos came to be,' Hesiod notes, but he does not tell us where and from what. Epicharmus, the Sicilian dramatist rightly objected to this: 'How can that be? It is impossible for a "first" thing to come from something and into something' (DK 23B1, Freeman 1983[1948] trans.). In case Chaos is indeed God (and Hesiod considers this so, naming it as a God of the underworld, a view taken up by Virgil and Seneca too), then it should lay no claims to beginning, since beginning by definition presupposes time and limit, both of which contradict the idea of the divine. If Chaos was truly divine, then it should have existed since time immemorial, or, to be precise, it should have always been inherent in the moment of the beginning. In case beginning is divine, then all further moments must be divine too; and since no moment can be started again or repeated, they are all moments of fulfilment as well. It was for this reason that the word *arche* signified control and domination, in addition to beginning (Heidegger 1978: 245). The beginning dominates what is in its wake, and since every moment is also a beginning, the beginning tends to rule over its own self first and foremost. In the case of the 'first' God, Chaos, this means that it is at once beginning and aftermath, master and servant, legitimate ruler and usurper—being simultaneously identical with its self and the absence of this self.

Chaos permeates everything, yet it cannot be caught out. There is Nothing that it could not bring to crisis point sooner or later.[7] It cannot be enclosed into limits, since it is chaos itself that sets existence into motion. It does not have a specific place, as it is lurking in everything. It is impossible to flee from it, since it is being revealed in everything—including the human being and the desire to flee.[8]

---

7 Existence is burdened with chaos, and beginning with the lack of beginning. The absence of domination leads to anarchy: the presence of a privative affix transforms *arche* into *anarchia*, anarchy—which equally signifies the lack of beginning (Parmenides, DK 28B8, 27) and confusion. 'Anarchy, show me a greater evil!' Creon points out to Haemon, using the term anarchy (Sophocles, *Antigone* 751–2). This refers not only to moral considerations (such as the duty towards the sovereign) but also to the tragic prescience of chaos, inherent in everything and only awaiting an opportunity to erupt.

8 The second-century BCE Ugaritic epic *Baal and Anath* presents Mavet (Mot), the chaotic God of death whom the Phoenicians considered to be the direct outcome of chaos's self-impregnation, as follows:

A lip to earth,
A lip to heaven,
And a tounge to the stars.

Mavet is later murdered by Anath, and then quartered, scorched and ground, so his ashes can be scattered on the fields new life to grow. The God of death is 'the core of the universe': there would be no life without him, yet everything that there is awaits its decay in its very throat. Hesiod describes a similar view: the roots, sources and limits of existence are to be found in the empty throat, the Tartarus. This is the entrance to the Underworld, a throat-like opening that not only emits but also draws in all that is alive: 'And there, all in their order, are the sources and ends of the dark earth and misty Tartarus and the unfruitful sea and starry heaven' (*Baal and Anath* 807–10). Krishna appears as a giant throat in the *Bhagavad Gita*, and when Arjuna asks him to appear in a divine guise in front of him, he fills up all the space between Heaven and Earth, and through his abyss-like throat the horrified mortal warrior is confronted with the whirling 'hell-hole' and crocodile throat of the universe:

Seeing Thy stupendous Form, O Most Mighty, with its myriad faces, its innumerable eyes and limbs and terrible jaws, I myself and all the worlds are overwhelmed with awe. When I see Thee, touching the Heavens, glowing with colour, with open mouth and wide open fiery eyes, I am terrified. O My Lord! My courage and peace of mind desert me. When I see Thy mouths with their fearful jaws like

It cannot be established where it will strike from, and cannot be tied down in time: it crops up in lightning-style moments when the allness of existence suddenly condenses into One. Such moments reveal a host of clefts criss-crossing existence, all pouring out, akin to a multitude of yawning throats, a sense of unappeasable absence. In moments of experiencing chaos, it becomes apparent that there resides a cavernous abyss in absolutely everything, from the thinnest sheets of paper to the sea, the sky, dried-out lava, the human glance, pain, desire, feeling, oblivion, or even boredom. Everything that there is, by virtue of mere existence tries to uphold itself, only to sink down into the bottomless vortex that has previously brought it up to the surface. Chaos is a form of absence that completes existence: through it, the all-vitalizing ungraspable can express its mutilating impact; hence, it is not really God but, rather, fear that infiltrates everything, and the impossible that continuously endeavours to undermine existence.

Attempts at Restraining Chaos

It is perfectly understandable that one attempts to shoo away the concept of chaos. One handles it as an object and distinguishes it from oneself, so one can thus point at it from afar and label it with

glowing fires at the dissolution of creation, I lose all sense of place; I find no rest. Be merciful, O Lord in whom this universe abides! All these sons of Dhritarashtra, with the hosts of princes, Bheeshma, Drona and Karna, as well as the other warrior chiefs belonging to our side; I see them all rushing headlong into Thy mouths, with terrible tusks, horrible to behold. Some are mangled between thy jaws, with their heads crushed to atoms. As rivers in flood surge furiously to the ocean, so these heroes, the greatest among men, fling themselves into Thy flaming mouths. As moths fly impetuously to the flame only to be killed, so these men rush into Thy mouths to court their own destruction. Thou seemest to swallow up the worlds, to lap them in flame. Thy glory fills the universe. Thy fierce rays beat down upon it irresistibly (*Bhagavad Gita* 11) names—and considers this essential in order to restrain it by enclosing it in the confines of rational discretion.

Attempts at 'restraining' chaos go back a long way. Labelling it as *space* or *amorphous matter* have made it utterable and comprehensible. The meaning of chaos was restricted to air space as long ago as the fifth century BCE (Kölscher 1968: 147). 'What lies between heaven and earth some call "chaos",' Euripides writes in his play *Cadmus* (*Bacchae* F448); and alluding to the fiery underworld river Phlegeton as well as to chaos, Virgil contends: 'wide silent *places* of the night' (*Aeneid* 6.265, emphasis added); and Ovid also likens chaos to 'fearful *places*' (*Metamorphoses* 10.29–30, emphasis added), a dark space beneath the Earth, with the Underworld set in opposition to the world above. According to these views, chaos is a place that can be 'charted', and that the individual can keep itself away from if exercising adequate circumspection.

An interpretation closer to the original character of chaos focuses on its messiness. Yet chaos is a *state* in this view, too, which precedes and perhaps also follows existence in its shapelessness, but which has no access to power at present. Like Hesiod, Virgil also presents Chaos as preceding everything else, so that earth, air, water and the kernel of fire derive from it (*Eclogues* 6.31–2). Ovid in particular draws attention to its disorderly matter:

> Before the ocean and the earth appeared—
> before the skies had overspread them all—
> the face of Nature in a vast expanse
> was naught but Chaos uniformly waste.
> It was a rude and undeveloped mass,
> that nothing made except a ponderous weight;
> and all discordant elements confused,
> were there congested in a shapeless heap.
>
> (*Metamorphoses* 1.5–10)

But while Hesiod posits Chaos as an omnipotent God, for the Romans *chaos* only has material qualities, in addition to which there is another non-material divine quality that, fed up with disorder, 'cut the land from skies, the sea from land' (ibid. 1.22). Hence chaos has limited power, as it is at the mercy of a God that has not been exposed to its touch.

In lieu of the All-Is-One paradox, there emerged the view centred on All-Is-Two: matter is perishable but the better half of our being, which is not of material origin, is non-perishable and everlasting. This view obviously fails to tackle the question that will subsequently overshadow Christianity too—namely: How can a non-divine chaos coexist with an almighty God, and why does good tolerate evil, and the timeless the time-bound? Ovid's reassuring hypothesis later found an audience in Christianity: the third- or fourth-century Gnostic text *Pistis Sophia* highlighted that Christ's truth is confronted with chaos, which remains untouched by this truth despite Christ having descended into the lowest regions (*topoi*) of chaos itself (*Pistis Sophia*, chap. 60). Later, in the thirteenth century, Saint Bonaventure draws on Ovid when he calls chaos mere raw material from which God created the world: *mixtum completum*, a blend of simple material elements (Bonaventure 1885: 300a). For Saint Thomas of Aquinas, it is also obvious that God surpasses chaotic ur-matter (*materia prima*) that lacks shape: 'matter is higher than accident, for matter is part of substance. But God can effect that accident exist without substance, as in the Sacrament of the Altar. He could, therefore, cause *matter to exist without form*' (*Summa Theologica* 66.1, emphasis added). Paracelsus is of the opinion that chaos is *materia prima*, wherefrom God created and then separated the four elements (Paracelsus 1968: 91). Much later, Kant also insists on the materiality of chaos: he observes in *Universal Natural History and Theory of the Heavens* that this was the ur-matter (*Grundstoff*, *Grundmaterie*), 'scattering of the elements of all materials throughout the entire extent of space' (2008: 22) that is as close as possible to 'Nothing', and in which state 'Nature, on the immediate edge of creation, was as raw and undeveloped as possible' (ibid.: 43). Chaos is mere matter in this case, which is simply shaped and untouched by divine intervention.

Yet if chaos is indeed separate from God, then it is truly mysterious. If it is eternal, then why is it not divine? Can two eternal and omnipotent Gods coexist side by side? If not, then where did chaos actually come from and how did it come about? Perhaps from Nothingness, with the aim of gradually making Nothingness seep into existence?

Compressing the Circle to a Dot

The materiality of chaos is an idea that became untenable around the age of Romanticism—at a time when the belief in God's omnipotence had also started to falter. Schelling—albeit in old age—passionately rejects the principle of material chaos. Chaos, he writes, is not 'a coarse mixture of material elements', not a formless and shapeless matter but a higher concept of metaphysical nature (1856: 35). He departs from the initial meaning of the word (to absorb, swallow up, yawn), which he interprets as follows: 'The word contains the notion of retreating into the deep, of being flung open, of opening up, which can be connected to the superior notion of giving up on resistance. The negative connotations of the former are further conveyed by the fact that the same word denotes the concept of need and necessity' (ibid.: 596). Following the logic of Schelling's philosophy of congeniality, this necessity and absence could also be called completeness: chaos cannot be classed as mere confusion or disorder by virtue of its lack of determination (including lack of confusion); it is thus sameness that precedes everything—in other words, it is original unity. Chaos, for Schelling is 'the metaphysical unity of rational potentials', which has not yet been split into different beings (ibid.: 600); it is nought (0) that contains both plus (+) and minus (-), at this stage indistinguishable from one another. Consequently, its most fitting symbol is the dot which has not yet stretched into a circle: 'the dot is a circle in state of chaos, or a circle perceived as chaotic' (ibid.).

Yet, this idea also has its Achilles' heel. When relating to chaos as a circle compressed to a dot, one loses sight of an essential quality that the philosopher himself has repeatedly alluded at: absence and inscrutability. In Schelling's view, chaos is an ideal state: it is from therein that all that exists—material and otherwise—spreads out, and it is thereto that they will later return; but as long as there is such a thing as existence, one can only talk about the *idea* of chaos. 'The word denotes a purely philosophical notion' (ibid.: 597), he notes in a logical outcome of his argument, and thus he also rejects the idea of chaos as an original vortex. Indeed, chaos threatens existence by being compressed into a dot; yet it also takes care of the expansion of the dot. Therefore, it cannot be reduced to a state of origin or finish; chaos is rather a pulsating force. Upon hearing the word chaos, one becomes spontaneously alert; its peculiar force resides in the mystery that it is both incomprehensible and experiential; it can amplify vitality and intensify each and every moment. This mystery cannot be solved: chaos permeates existence as a whole, from the tiniest speck of dust or batting of an eyelid, through passion and confusion, to the structure and stillness of the universe; yet chaos itself can never be caught in the act. It is something that cannot even be identified as Something, seeing that it is omnipresent and so profuse.

Chaos cannot be likened to anything—at most it resembles *the* Nothing that, despite the fact that it does not exist, tends to be frequently spoken of. Chaos is 'the non-being that, as a potential, acted as a model for this visible universe', observes Franz von Baader, a contemporary of Schelling, who is often remembered as 'Boehmius redivivus' for his tireless work as Jakob Böhme's exegete (Letter to Jacobi, 3 January 1798; Baader 1851–60: VOL. 15, 177). In this view, it is not chaos that comprises plus and minus, but the other way round: chaos comes to life as a result of the conflict between the two. Chaos manifests itself—'exists'—by virtue of charging existence with its own absence. It backs out of everything, which is why it can only be 'caught in the act' via tension—in tense and touching moments, which appear utterly grave despite the gaping absence in their wake. Chaos, this named guise of the impossible, cannot be restricted to a particular point, state, situation or time. It is latent in everything and illuminates a peculiar quality of the universe: namely, that although it exists, it could also exist not—to use a grammatically incorrect turn. 'The total character of the world [. . .] is in all eternity chaos,' (1974: 168), contends Nietzsche, adding: 'I say to you: one must still have chaos in oneself in order to give birth to a dancing star' (2006: 9). Chaos reigns over everything. It nestles into the individual too, and it cannot be ousted because it has also made its way into the human heart.

The Abyss of Nothingness

Chaos resides in everything, yet it only manifests its own absence. This thought is not new; Böhme has already formulated it earlier, although he expressed this in relation to God, not chaos. For Empedocles, it is the everlasting whirlabout of love and hate, while for Böhme, the whirling of Heaven and Hell that perpetuates and destroys everything: it is these two poles that interpenetrate, always and everywhere. Yet Böhme never fails to posit God as the ultimate point of reference, and his predilection for universal drama is always stronger than the compulsion to fully clarify everything. Thus, God becomes for him a whirling force and a *chaotic* foundation, despite a lack of adequate explanation in this sense.

> This ground is called Mysterium Magnum, or a chaos, because good and evil arise out of it, viz. light and darkness, life and death, joy and grief, salvation and damnation. For it is the ground of souls and angels, and of all eternal creatures, evil as well as good; it is a ground of heaven and

hell, also of the visible world, and all that is therein [. . .].
Yet we cannot say that the spiritual world has had any
beginning, but has been manifested from eternity out of
that chaos (Böhme 2019: 50–2).

This chaotic foundation that 'underbids' everything is itself
unfounded: according to Böhme, this is the abyss that is God's
actual 'foundation', 'the eye of the abyss, the eternal chaos' (1910:
chap. 1). This eye casts a glance everywhere, and looks back onto
everything. Yet the term 'bottomless abyss' is more than just a
metaphor for Böhme, as it also was for Schelling and Baader: all
three use this term to translate what was known by the cabbalists
as *en sof* or *ensoph*, with which they aimed to convey the infinite
and inconceivable quality of God. In *De Arte Cabalistica* (1517),
Johann Reuchlin observed: 'Not even our thought can grasp him,
he who is called *En Sof*—"Infinity" [. . .] hidden away in the fur-
thest recesses of his divinity, into the unreachable abyss of the fountain of light [. . .]. He is being and non-being—all that to our
rational minds seems contrary and self-contradictory' (1983: 121).
En sof is beyond description; and earlier cabbalists likened it to
Nothingness for the very reason to suggest the close connection
between existence and the divine Nothingness.

Gershom Scholem draws attention to the fact that although *en
sof* makes 'Nothingness' appear, this does not imply non-Being but
storm, drama and vortex. The Nothingness comprised in *en sof* is
'the abyss and *Ungrund* hidden in the absolute Nothingness of
which we have only a vague intimation' (1990: 443) The bottom of
this abyss cannot be seen, just as one cannot catch a glimpse of the
bottom of the vortex either. In moments of intense experience,
Man's entire being transforms into a vortex, turning into a chaotic
being who will be 'the eye of the bottomless abyss'. This reveals the
crack through which everything that there is can be charged up
with the invisible foundation of its own self—or, to put it differently,
with chaotic absence.

Depths and Heights

The experience of the 'bottomless abyss' also leads to the recognition of a peculiar truth, even if this truth does not offer any tangible knowledge. Democritus argues that 'We know nothing in reality; for truth lies in an abyss' (DK 68B117, Freeman 1983[1948] trans.). *Ho bythos*, he observes in relation to the location of truth, which means depths as well as the bottom of the sea (in Greek mosaics, Bythos was often represented as a monster). Yet this term refers not only to spatial depth but also to its absence, a sense of spaceless unfulfilled-ness.[9] According to the teachings of the Gnostic Valentinus, the perfect eternal reigns in the invisible and unnameable heights, and precedes (*proonta*) existence itself—he calls this *height depth* (*bythos*), ur-beginning (*proarche*) and ur-father (*propater*) (Schultz 1986: 164). In this sense depth is not spatial, since it can also be expressed in terms of height. The author of an early Gnostic work, aiming to convey the unsurpassable quality of the father of the universe, contends that he was surrounded by 12 depths; Plotinus, who could not be blamed for holding Gnostic views, notes that God embraces everything into his hold yet lives in the lower depths (*en bathei*) (*Enneads* 6.8.18); and the ninth-century Irish philosopher Scotus Erigena claims that we can only talk about *the depths* of divine essence because it is endowed with inconceivable *height* and limitlessness (1987: 2.17).

The Church attempted 'to tame' this chaotic depth, just like the Romans tried to tame chaos by calling it of spatial and material origin. In his debates with the Gnostics in the second century, Irenaeus objected to the fact that, while his opponents considered *bythos* as

---

9 Pindar uses this word derived from the Indo-Germanic root *dheu-* when discussing the all-engulfing, crocodile-throated depth of the Tartarus (*Odes* 4.44); the old Welsh term *annwf(y)n* can also be traced back to this root, meaning the realm of the dead and the Gods; and so can the Gallic *dubno*, meaning world. The deepness, the throat of chaos is never too far: it permeates the world, and is the world itself.

the foundation-less foundation of the universe, they expanded it to such an extent that in the process it has become deprived of existence. He is confident that the unknown God, who would occasionally be venerated even with altars built in his honour, is not Bythos, the ur-being invented by the Gnostics, but an invisible father, the creator of the world. In his view, God, 'as regards His greatness, is indeed unknown to all [. . .]; but as regards His love, He is always known through Him by whose means He ordained all things' (*Against Heresies* 4.20.4, quoted by Norden 1913: 75).

According to this view, the absence of the abyss may unsettle but does not really deceive the individual: God does not allow one to fall victim to chaos and fathomless depth. Chaos has often been associated with the underworld, and depth awaits a similar fate. Bythos, and *abythos* (*abyssos*) as place names and nouns represent the kingdom of the dead for Diogenes Laërtius (*Lives and Opinions of Eminent Philosophers* 4.5.27); in his epistles to the Romans, Paul calls the underworld *abyssos* (Romans 10:7); for Peter, this place is reserved for fallen angels (2 Peter 2:4); and in the Book of Revelation, this is Hell where the dragon, the ur-serpent or, in other words, the devil resides (Revelation 20:2). Following this, Church fathers likened the *abyssos* not only to Hell or *Infernum* but also to chaos and, in this way, handed control over chaotic depths to God, rather than attempting to search for a rift in the supposed God itself.

The Foundation

And yet, fathomless depth cannot be demarcated by limits. The ultimate 'foundation', in case we can even presume its existence, is not a limit or an extreme point but the whirling abyss itself, complete with depth and dazzle.

The foundation, as a particular notion of mysticism, generally signifies the presence of God that surpasses existence. As Johann Tauler, a contemporary of Meister Eckhart, observes: 'The depth that is in God is an abyss that no created mind can fathom' (1909: 530). It is the undoubtedly Christian bias of mysticism that comes to fore when, despite its incomprehensibility, Tauler considers this 'divine foundation' as a form of fulfilment. Yet when one loses one's footing in 'timeless' moments, one becomes aware of the fact that one's being is saturated with chaos—and this characterizes both tragic and joyful moments. In such instances, one not only finds 'fulfilment' but also loses oneself. A German expression illuminates this paradox most fittingly: *zu Grunde gehen* literally means 'to go back to the foundation', but its actual meaning is to perish.[10] According to Heidegger, only the existent, only be-ing beings have a foundation (*Grund*); and because Being cannot have such a thing since everything else is founded on it, when he talks about the 'foundation' of Being, he adds a privative affix *Abgrund*—that is, abyss (1957: 93).[11]

In crushing moments of the so-called divine experience, one becomes aware of this very abyss. This dominates the entire existence—this is the abyss that lies right ahead of the individual, even if one can only see mountains or plains.[12] This is the whirling chaos, the perfect 'embodiment' of which, in rare and isolated moments, is the human being itself.

---

10 'What perishes [*zu Grunde geht*] does not make it to or into God but, rather, the Devil', observes Baader (1851–60: VOL. 14, 117). In this case, Devil is the unfulfillable absence of existence.

11 The word 'foundation' in German (*Grund*) can be supplied with two different privative affixes: *Abgrund* and *Ungrund*. According to Baader, *Abgrund* is the outermost point in relation to God; *Ungrund*, the innermost (ibid.: VOL. 7, 303).

12 '[A]nd where doth man not stand at abysses! Is not seeing itself—seeing abysses?' (Nietzsche 1999: 107)

CHAPTER 6

THE IMPOSSIBLE

Cornelis van Poelenburg, *Portrait of a Young Girl*, fragment

'I am from eternity to eternity, outside me is nothing except what is something merely through my will; *but whence then am I?*'— God asks in Kant's *Critique of Pure Reason* (1998: 574). Who else could he turn to but us, albeit we are even more at our wits' end than him. Is it our fallibility that he confides in? Does he crave the fruit of our ignorance? Does he want to sin? He must definitely be aware that human ruin was brought about by a longing for 'divine' knowledge. Was not God's reason for casting off the first human pair to ensure that they fail to realize that divine knowledge in fact consists of a torrent of unanswerable questions? Yet it now seems as if God had had enough of himself, too. He would like to submerge into the very vortex that would redeem him from his own self. He would rather become mortal, so he could also pin his hopes on something and believe in another God.

Yet could he even raise such questions if he was not afraid of his own death? Besides, would he even be a God if he was not surrounded by the haunting of mortality? Is he not given the kiss of life by the nothing that occasionally flashes out of the human gaze like lightning?

Whoever asks questions, is God. Yet their questions may also turn out to be an affirmation that is uttered through the mouth of death.

[D]eath is not the pathos of the ultimate human possibility, the possibility of impossibility, but the ceaseless repetition of what cannot be grasped, before which the I loses its ipseity. The impossibility of possibility [. . .]. In death [. . .] the regular order is reversed, since, in it, power leads to what is unassumable. Thus the distance between life and death is infinite. [. . .] Death is not the end, it is the never-ending ending.

Emmanuel Levinas (1996: 132)

Até, the Banished God

In Greek mythology, Até (or Aite) was the Goddess of misfortune, damnation and delusion. She was one of the most frequently mentioned Gods—hardly a moment would go by without someone calling her name. In fact, few people could claim that Até had never crossed their paths. Hence, it is striking that no visual representation has survived of this Goddess who embodies misfortune. Her presence must have been so closely entwined with people's fates that it turned out to be impossible to isolate her figure by means of artistic portrayal. At first, Até lived on Mount Olymp and picked her victims from among the Gods. She did not even spare Zeus, and this proved to be her downfall. Prior to the birth of Heracles, she nestled into Zeus' soul, who in his impaired vision announced that the first child to be born would rule over all others. Having first made Zeus swear an oath that he would keep his promise, Hera hastened to Argos and, while delaying the birth-giving of Alchmene, the mother of Heracles, assisted with the premature birth of Eurystheos, son of Nikippe and grandson of Pelops. Zeus could not go back on this oath; but in his rage he yanked Até's hair and threw her off Mount Olymp, into the midst of mortal humans from where she could never return (Homer, *Iliad* 9.95–103). From then on, Até would search for victims among the humans, dazzling one person after the other. Her feet would never touch the ground, since she would reside in the soul and spirit of her future victims (Plato, *Symposium* 195d). No wonder that no one had ever seen or confronted her: she lived in people's hearts, and as a result, it was near impossible to picture her.

Like Eros, Até could also only be noticed when it was too late: hence, it should not take us by surprise that both have a tendency to dazzle people. Até, however, does not only dazzle mortals but also sows the seeds of discord among them. Her name originates from the Indo-Germanic *uā-*, *uō-*, *u-* root, which connotes disaster and wounding. Nestling herself into the soul, Até dazzles people; since they can no longer sense the origin of trouble, they throw caution to the wind and engage in brawling. Falling victim to Até, the individual loses itself; and despite subsequently blaming the Goddess for its state, one never manages to cast a glance on her. One enters into conflict with one's own self, and as a result, can at most recognize God in one's own alienated self. In such states of bedazzlement, it is the human being that transforms into Até, and partakes of an experience akin to that of the banished God: excluded from the realm of the immortals and flung into transience.

One is able to draw closer to God, but as Até exemplifies, this tends to happen when getting into conflict with oneself and experiencing one's own misfortune. Até's figure is this vague because she is too close to humans for anyone to reveal or paint her.

God is that imaginable utmost limit which, in moments of the so-called divine experience, is revealed as the limitless. The experience of limitlessness does not allow one to reconcile with one's own finitude. This fuels the urge to become divine in order to become limitless (that is immortal), but since this cannot be realized in practice, *God enters the human mind as the epitome of the impossible.* Yet this impossible cannot be reduced to something that is unrealizable. We are not simply dealing with a practical unrealizability, which might prompt one towards a rational exercise of discretion (one can easily give up on putting a bare hand into fire, attempting to swim across the sea, or taking off by way of flapping the arms), but with an incentive force that does not allow one to settle for anything at all. This force gives wings, and inspires rather than urges to back down. Plutarch observes in relation to Alexander the Great that he turned out to represent 'woe and great calamity' (até) for Asia (*Alexander* 3.4): he embodied a force that opposed the universe itself, and defied existence as a whole. (No wonder that Altdorfer's painting of the battle of Issus [in the Alte Pinakothek, Munich], which depicts the armies of Darius and Alexander as a single bubbling vortex absorbing both the horizon and the blazing sky, later became Napoleon's favourite: in 1800 he seized it and displayed it in his bathroom in Saint-Cloud.) This stimulating force confronts the individual with what surpasses it by way of the limitless, and this makes it, on the one hand, realize that it can only have access to one, and only one, life and, on the other, unable to resign to this fate. The apparition of the *divine* fractures the seeming peace of the world, and the impossible begins its expansion in the human.

Até was exiled from Mount Olymp, yet she acted as an envoy for Zeus and as the messenger of the incomprehensible. Writing about Até's 'place', Empedocles names all those who live there: earthwoman and wide-eyed sunwoman, gory feud and stern-gazed unity, in other words, harmony, beauty and ugliness, speed and slowness, kind truth and black-eyed confusion, as well as the figures of 'Growth and Decay, Rest and Waking, Movement and Immobility, much-crowned Majesty, and Defilement, Silence and Voice' (DK 31B122–3, Freeman 1983[1948] trans.). Having surveyed all of the above, the philosopher heaves a sigh: 'Alas, oh wretched race of mortals, direly unblessed! Such are the conflicts and groanings from which you have been born!' (ibid., B124). Até's realm is limitless; it encompasses everything since even deniers of this world are subject to her power. She keeps watch over origin and decay, and it is of no concern to her whether mortals want to be given birth, or would like to circumvent death. As Plato's uncle, the sophist Critias contended: 'Nothing is certain, except that having been born we die, and that in life one cannot avoid disaster' (DK 88B49, Freeman 1983[1948] trans.).

One becomes aware of the limitations of one's depressing life once Ate moves into one's soul. In such instances one experiences oneself as a banished God and, as a result, finds oneself bedazzled and tends to perceive life as a giant wound. When translating *Antigone* into German, Hölderlin's infallible intuition opted for madness (*Wahnsinn*) to render Até's name (Wahnsinn).[1] He did not mean to suggest mental illness, but a state that surpasses sobriety, as his comments on the translation demonstrate: 'holy madness' is 'the highest human trait', and this 'surpasses' all other hypostases of mankind (1952: 267).[2]

Até drives humans 'mad', which leads to everything appearing as one entity: one perceives darkness in light, paralysing stillness in speed, filth in splendour, discord in unity and, as a foundation

---

1 Glückselige solcher Zeit, da man nicht schmecket das Übel;
  Denn, wenn sich reget von Himmlischen
  Einmal ein Haus, fehlts dem an Wahnsinn nicht,
  In der Folge, wenn es Sich mehrt
  (*Antigone* 604–08)

The English translation opts for 'shaken': 'Fortunate is the man who has never tasted God's vengeance! / Where once the anger of heaven struck, that house is shaken' (Sophocles 1990: 273).

2 See the following lines from the poem 'Bread and Wine' (Hölderlin 2004), which illustrates the connections between madness and Platonic mania: 'Light-hearted madness, then, may well deride derision / When it takes hold, on the instant, of poets in sanctified night'.

to all these, decay in origin. Seeing everything-as-one, however, comes at the price of inner conflict, and one finds oneself experiencing a heightened sense of one's mortality. The urge to flee from one's own self is stronger than ever and everything, yet Até conceals herself even in this very impulse. One is possessed by a God that pushes one beside oneself over and over again, and, as a result, distorts into one's own worst enemy. Até reached her goal. Thereafter, her victim can only contemplate oneself in the mirror of their own decay.

The Impersonal God

Understandably, there are no visual representations of Até. The power attributed to her via mythological descriptions is limitless precisely because it is not connected to any one figure. Strictly speaking, 'Até' does not exist; it is merely the name of discord, which cannot be attached to any place and which manifests itself in a succession of random mortals. The power linked to Até can be experienced by anyone; but since this stirs up a universal discord in the individual, by becoming 'Até', one also partakes of an experience that situates one at the mercy of an omnipotent force. This force radiates from everything yet cannot be reduced to actual phenomena. In unsettling moments, when one is touched by chaos and, having transcended everything, perceives oneself as the divine centre, it rightly feels that one has also become a victim of discord. These moments are clear testimonies to the existence and might of the vortex as the ultimate evidence for genesis and decay.

Otherness

In moments of divine experience, when one finally becomes self-aware—and this can equally be a moment of rapture, an instance of Hölderlinian madness, disgust, crying, fear or sensual pleasure—an alien force starts to emerge in the background. As if one did not venture into the blind alley of passion out of one's own will but following orders from an unknown authority. Could one get alienated from oneself at the very point of approaching one's own long-anticipated centre?

These moments are sacred, even though they have nothing in common with what organized religion calls sacred. This is an anarchical sacredness: the unknown and alien trespasses into the familiar world in order to place it beside itself. Despite the fact that in a postmodern view Lacan's concept of the 'big Other' does not exist, according to two and a half thousand years of European cultural tradition—or at least up until mankind was a metaphysically inclined being—mankind experienced as sacred things that were radically different. As Sloterdijk puts it: 'Metaphysical asceticism is fundamentally a conscious elaboration on the incompatibility [between the individual and cosmos]. It amplifies the schism between the individual and its life so far, and gradually channels it into a realm where it becomes its own entirely Other, its actual object, and a proper Existent' (1993: 221). This Other, this manifestation of the sacred, cannot be approached in a gradual manner; the individual either gets lost in it in a daze or shows no awareness of it whatsoever. The sacred has always signified segregation: the Greek *hagios* has originally meant an enclosed area inaccessible to mortals; the Latin *sanctus* derives from the **sāg-* (encompass, enclose) root; and the Hebrew *gadôš* (holy) also hints at the idea of separation. One experiences the sacred if something perceived as alien and unconquerable moves into oneself and dazzles—in other words, if the *Other* is experienced as the *Same*. It is irrelevant whether this entails misery, as in pain, or pleasure, as in love; if this *Other* becomes so overpowering that it essentially ends up out of control, then one experiences the sacred even in situations where the actual *concept* of the sacred does not cross one's mind.

The world (*cosmos*) and the sacred (*hagios*) are confronting one another, claims an anonymous old Gnostic work (*Books of Jeu* 1978:

chap. 18). According to this view, the Alien and the Other have to take the upper hand for the individual to get to know itself and have its inner truth revealed. In sacred moments, one gets to one's inner self via the roundabout way of Otherness, initially moving away from oneself. Hence the expression 'losing oneself', since in such situations one is alienated from everything, including oneself. In moments of shock, one experiences the contradictory dynamic of existence: experiencing fulfilment, despite finding oneself permeated by an irresolvable sense of alienation at the same time. Every historical period has encountered this alienation of the world from itself; however, few have taken on board the devastating force inherent in this experience. Relevant in this respect are the Gnostics, who interpreted alienation as a synonym for the so-called trans- or hypercosmic, and experienced an unsurmountable abyss between earthly existence and the alien and unknowable God in charge of this existence (Schultz 1986: 51);[3] those among the early Christians who periodically evoked the idea of total Otherness relative to God (Otto 1936: 1), until the Church has finally 're-established' unity, stating that God may be unknown but not unknowable;[4] or the mystics who favoured *individual* experience over the *shared* path indicated by the Church, and gave voice to the experience of unstoppable alienation.[5] Nietzsche can also be included in this line-up, since he stressed the importance of the heavenly Nothing, inaccessible and devoid of humans; or E. M. Cioran, who drew conclusions on the botching of creation based on the abundance of alienation present in the world; or Georges Bataille, who built his

---

3 "We are not of his world, and the world is not of us, either,' a prayer from Qatar contends (Schultz 1986: 53).

4 '[A]s regards His greatness, is indeed unknown to all [. . .]; but as regards His love, He is always known through Him by whose means He ordained all things,' Irenaeus observes (Irenaeus of Lyons, *Against Heresies* 4.20.4, quoted in Norden 1913: 75).

5 'Tell between me and God the only difference? / It is (put in one word) nothing but otherness' (Silesius 1986: 66).

theoretical world on *Otherness*, that is to say on *heterology* (*heteros* = the other),[6] thus reviving a Gnostic tradition, seeing that one of their central concepts was *heteros*.

Dead Ends

Where does the stubbornly recurrent experience of alienation and Otherness in European intellectual tradition come from?

Lautréamont's *The Songs of Maldoror* includes the following passionate lament:

> It is obvious that, at least during the day, anyone can put up useful resistance against the Great Exterior Object (who does not know his name?); for then the will ensures its own defence with remarkable ferocity. But as soon as the veil of nocturnal vapours spreads, even over condemned men about to be hanged—oh! to see one's intellect in a stranger's sacrilegious hands [. . .] Humiliation! Our door is open to the fierce curiosity of the Celestial Bandit. I have not deserved this infamous torment, you hideous spy of my causality! If I exist, I am not another. I do not admit this equivocal plurality in me [. . .] My subjectivity and the Creator—it is all too much for one brain (2011: 5.3).

Lautréamont claims that the most 'ignoble punishment' is the one experienced by humans, namely, that one is unable to be in charge over the only thing that is the sole evidence of one's existence: one's own life. For the individual, the 'Other' is not a concept, not a theoretical concern, but a sense of alienation that confronts one with one's own decay. One has become the recipient of the sole

---

6 'Violence, excess, delirium, madness characterize heterogeneous elements to varying degrees: active, as persons or mobs, they result from breaking the laws of social homogeneity [. . .] compared to everyday life, heterogeneous existence can be represented as something other, as incommensurate, by charging these words with the positive value they have in affective experience' (Bataille 1997: 127–8).

thing one can identify with, one's own life, without having been consulted whether one wants this or not, and this life is taken away similarly without consultation. The 'Other' is the expression of the impossibility that everything that there is, mankind included, owes its origin to something that is not identical with itself. Every existence is charged with its own absence; in everything that there is, something Other is also inherently nestled, so that it can sooner or later annihilate the existent without risking to also destroy itself.

When Até, the Goddess of discord, is personified in the human being, one experiences life as the impossible, and as a miracle that one exists at all, since one could not exist just as well. The impossible in which one finds oneself in moments of divine experience cannot be eluded; and one finds oneself in the grips of alienation because this impossible cannot be realized in any way, it cannot be 'charged' with any possibility, and the sense of absence it generates cannot be relieved by any positive content. And yet, in the process of being touched by the impossible, one does not yield to resignation but experiences a sense of infinite power. One's entire being is taken over by a single mighty yes—even in situations whereby this manifests in all-encompassing negation. The impossible allows us to cast a glimpse into the contradictory nature of existence, whereby one both rules over and is subservient to oneself. Through existence, one is the depositary of a 'Being' that guarantees all existence; at the same time, as an individual condemned to decay, one also has to endure the impossibility of this 'Being'. The impossible, therefore, is not a noun, and is no equivalent to God, as proposed by theologians, or to Being, as perceived by ontologists. It is not an attribute either, since in this case it would have to be assigned to something that by definition would restrain its all-permeating power. The very usage of the word is misleading, since we are dealing with something that should not in fact be called impossible; a hyphen (-), free-standing brackets () or three dots (. . .) would better illustrate this concept than words. In cathartic moments, it is this that supplants everything else from one's field of vision, and compels the individual to experience its entire life as a random hyphen or some brackets that cannot be placed into a broader referential context.

The Impossible: Negative Affirmation

One of the main aims of the European tradition starting with Plato and culminating with Christianity was to equip the individual to handle the temptation of the impossible. This process is fundamentally ideological (the concept of ideology as such appeared in the course of the Enlightenment, and the term was coined by Destutt de Tracy in the eighteenth century). Ideology teaches about the idea, or, to put it differently, about the sensorially visible. One can only see what one faces up to, and what is identical with the self remains unseen, akin to the eyeball that cannot catch sight of itself. If detachment from God is considered to be a sin, then ideology itself is an indication of 'failure': despite their best efforts, ideologists tend to betray and forget about the very thing they are most eager to promote.

> Ever since being got interpreted as idea, thinking about the being of beings has been metaphysical, and metaphysics has been theological. In this case theology means the interpretation of the 'cause' of beings as God and the transferring of being onto this cause, which contains being in itself and dispenses being from out of itself, because it is the being-est of beings (Heidegger 1998b: 181).

The concept of an existence perceived as an object that can be named shuts down communication with the impossible latent in everything, and so does a named or imagined concept of God with divine experience.

By seeking an explanation for everything, ideologists find themselves attempting to leave aside the impossible, this defining characteristic of existence. In parallel with this and as a counter-reaction of sorts, European cultural tradition has always entertained the idea to reclaim God—albeit at the price of deicide (Nicolaus Cusanus / Nicholas of Cusa, Pascal, Nietzsche). Scotus Erigena observed in the ninth century:

> For everything that is understood and sensed is nothing else but the apparition of what is not apparent, the manifestation of the hidden, the affirmation of the negated, the comprehension of the incomprehensible, [the utterance of the unutterable, the access to the inaccessible], the understanding of the unintelligible, the body of the bodiless, the essence of the superessential, the form of the formless, the measure of the measureless, the number of the unnumbered, the weight of the weightless, the materialization of the spiritual, the visibility of the invisible, the definition of the infinite, the circumscription of the uncircumscribed (1987: 3.4.633A–B; p. 250).

According to this quote, everything is but the semblance of another underlying thing. In moments of divine experience, it comes to light that this underlying thing is nowhere to be found, this being the most visible semblance. Thus, Erigena claims nothing less than that *everything that exists makes being visible; however, through this very process of representation/visualization, being also finds itself concealed.*

Those who did not want to hand over divine experience to theism and the Church tried to rescue a sense of the personal God by utilising the method of negative theology and rejected the concept of God as an ideological and tyrannical figure that towers over existence. The followers of Plotinus[7] did not find the concept of an accomplished UNITY satisfactory, and, by way of complex systems, arrived at the idea of UNITY ABOVE UNITY (Iamblichus), which

---

7 Plotinus—according to Porphyry (*On the Life of Plotinus* 23)—partook of divine experience (meaning ecstatic rapture) on four occasions in his life.

already contains the haunting seeds of negation. The Gnostics made a point of layering privative affixes so that THE UNNAMABLE cannot be tied down in a name, and THE UNGRASPABLE cannot solidify into an object. Later, Damascius writes about THE UNUTTERABLE, Dionysius the Areopagite about BEING BEYOND ALL, Scotus Erigena about NOTHING, and Symeon the New Theologian about THE INVIS-IBLE LIGHT and brings the orphic NIGHT to life. PURE DIVINE SPIRIT is a recurrent phrase for Meister Eckhart, whereas THE ETERNAL UNCREATED NOTHING and UNUTTERABLE HIDDENNESS regularly occur in Tauler's work. Influenced by the Kabbalah's EN SOPH, Böhme discusses the BOTTOMLESS ABYSS, and Baader NOTHING and EVERYTHING. In the spirit of the Brahman-Hindu ATMAN, Schelling talks about WORLD SPIRIT, Schleiermacher about the INFINITE, and the young Hegel about PURE LIFE. The paradox that fuels privative affixes is inherent in Hölderlin's thoughts on tragedy seen as an UR-PARADOX, and in Goethe's mysterious notion of the DEMONIC, that is not divine, human, diabolic or angelic, and that 'it seemed only to accept the impossible and scornfully to reject the possible' (Goethe 1908: part 4, chap. 20). In the twentieth century, J. E. Harrison, Rudolf Otto, Roger Caillois and Mircea Eliade postulate on the notion of paradoxical SACREDNESS, with reference to reli-gions from outside Europe, and Heidegger attempts to rescue BEING from the clutches of theological definitions. In his old age, Heidegger finds even this terminology inadequate, and chooses to spell it with the letters crossed out: B̶E̶I̶N̶G̶; while Artaud, obsessed with the notion of all-consuming DEATH, considers pain as the raw material of existence. Negation after negation. Despite the fact that all-encompassing negation should in principle feed into knowledge, moments of shock tend to lead to a monumental affirmation. In moments of divine experience, speech is distorted by a multitude of privative suffixes; and yet, the countless *nos* join together as a single *yes*. Getting closer to one's self, the individual discovers oneself in the impossible. In such cases, one does not say yes to particular things, but to something that permeates one's entire inner being despite making oneself intangible to one's own self. According to Heidegger, Being 'enlightens', and heading that way the individual also becomes enlightened. Yet the faces of those who are carried away by passion and who are silenced by the impossible accumulating therein, betray that there is something in them that deprives one of the hope in the 'ultimate' enlightenment. In such moments, one actually says yes to the impossible itself.

Still, can one run the risk of any affirmation of the very thing that makes everything impossible? In moments of utter shock, is it actually the human being that says yes to the impossible? Is it not the other way round? Is not one just the mouthpiece of the impossible? Is it not the impossible that actually says yes to the human being, merely tolerating its existence?

In the Labyrinth

The individual is a *one-off* being despite the fact that *all*-upholding existence is manifest in each and every fiber of its body; basically, one owes one's life to something that is fundamentally foreign. One's facial features are unmistakeable, and yet, these unique features would not exist without the contribution of the entire cosmos; one's body is exclusively one's own, despite not finding oneself any closer to it than to planets light years away; the growth of hair or nails are events on a par with the explosion of stars; bodily fluids are raw materials of the universe itself; heartbeat is nourished by the all-engulfing and all-emitting silence; and the darkness filling up one's body is fuelled by the universal invisible. Everything that there is shares the fate of all others: they embody and are at the mercy of the force that pulsates therein. This force makes it possible for them to exist, and therefore surpasses existence; yet this force is also something that belongs to the realm of the non-existing and is hence left behind. Bataille's short story entitled 'The Impossible' deliberately uses the obscure phrase 'that, that is' (*ce qui est*) in order to denote the all-encompassing and vitalizing immeasurable, 'the totality in which man has his share by losing himself' (1997: 269). Yet not even a phrase like 'limitless totality' is capable of rendering what it should convey. Bataille himself observes elsewhere that regarding 'that, that is': 'I know nothing, absolutely nothing. But I know: "non-knowledge communicates ecstasy"' (ibid.: 88). Thus, the phrase 'that, that is' finds itself undermined by what these words are directed at, and it would in fact be more accurate to say THAT, THAT IS NOT WHAT IT IS. In the course of divine experience, it emerges that one—as a habitual Godseeker—searches for God in vain, as the road leading thereto is infinite. In order to find God, one has to first find one's own self and see oneself face to face, from an external perspective, in one's entirety and unity. This road is akin to an infinite spiral, since one would not only have to be able to see one's own unified self but also encompass one's external observer I as well, and then integrate into this one-ness the 'superior'—or, rather, 'inferior'—all-comprising I, and so on and so forth. And yet, entering this labyrinth one rightly senses approaching one's own self and has finally started to lead one's very own life. This life is just as immeasurable and inconceivable as the universe, as 'that, that is'. When one experiences that the universe is not a neutral object that can be opposed, and discovers the latter's intrinsic and alien nature in one's own self, then it partakes of the impossible and transforms into a subject of the universe. In such situations, one realizes that the most one can say about oneself is 'not the one either': one's life, body and soul are captive to a vortex that, in a rare moment, had one crystallized from non-existent into existent, with a view to, later, get one annihilated again.

Poetry

In moments of divine experience, it comes to light that God, as the subject of theology, does not even exist, and a personal God first has to die in order to resurrect. Nothing can be said of the God of theologians (since Nothing cannot be articulated),[8] or in case humans insist on talking about this God, one finds oneself under the necessity of enclosing it into a 'profane' (in other words, desecrated) verb–predicate structure.[9] By contrast, the *experienced* God attempts to exit the human being at all costs; in moments of divine experience, one does not speak by virtue of one's own free will but is prompted to speak by the God inherent therein. This is the God that makes language explode in order to open up the passage towards the impossible. 'It is only in inspired terms that the divine can be spoken of,' the young Hegel writes (1971: 255) at a time when he is still committed to the idea of the impossible. Enthusiasm by definition is a saturation with soul (*pneuma*); *enthusiasmus* literally means that the human being is saturated with God. In such cases, one not only begins to distance oneself from one's hitherto known I, but from the language at one's disposal, too. Instead of separating subject and predicate, which in itself betrays a vulnerable situation of sorts (as a subject, the individual distinguishes itself from the universe, and attempts to coerce into object-position all that surpasses it), one becomes both object and predicate to one's own subject. Language turning impossible indicates that one has found oneself in 'that, that is' (and loses oneself in 'that, that is not'), and through language use, one takes part in its immeasurability.

This protrusion of the impossible should in principle lead to silence. At the same time, this is a precondition of poetry, too—although all poetry, nurtured by the impossible, incorporates

---

8 Rudolf Otto observes: 'These terms, supernatural and transcendent [. . .] give the appearance of positive attributes, and, as applied to the mysterious, they appear to divest the mysterium of its originally negative meaning and to turn it into an affirmation' (1936: 30).

9 'But beings can be experienced as objects only where human beings have become subjects, those who experience their fundamental relation to beings as the objectification—understood as mastery—of what is encountered' (Heidegger 1998a: 189).

the silence conjured up by Hamlet's final words. Within poets, the universe becomes subjective; they experience a heightened sense of alienation from their own being (since they recognize themselves in what is not them: the cosmic unity, and in the Other), but this is fuelled by the same alienation that permeates existence as a whole. Alienated from its own self, the poet 'finds the way home' and settles into the impossible. This places them beside themselves; yet also persuades them to recognize in everything their fellow sufferer: in stones, animals, faraway planets as well as, say, the air. This invisible unity transpires not only in poetry but also in music and painting. Music provides 'the only unembodied form of access *to the world of higher knowledge* [. . .], that surrounds mankind but which remains outside its grasp,' Beethoven notes in a letter (quoted in Bergfleth 1987: 61). Poetry becomes authentic when poets—musicians or painters—not only point out the intangible but also touch it, and not only hint at the impossible but also throw themselves on its mercy.

A work of art is not powerful by virtue of what the poet utters, the composer notates, the painter paints or the sculptor sculpts, but by virtue of what surrounds these words, notes, brushstrokes and forms. A work becomes arresting by virtue of being in the predatory grips of the indescribable, inexpressible and unmouldable. It is not only the work but also its beholder that find themselves in these grips, since a work produces more elemental impact, the more it 'provokes' the inexpressible and confronts the recipient with what is 'non human' in its self. Every work attempts to surpass itself: it tries to capture and mould into shape the very essence that ensures the existence of form itself. This hopeless struggle illustrates that there is no work that would be entirely satisfactory; and they are likely to get greater (deeper, more moving and seductive), the more one senses that it was the impossible that has actually prompted them.

A work of art comes to life in the absence of peace; the artist would not be compelled to create if the world was in unison with itself, and the artist with the world. Supposedly indissoluble harmony (the ultimate human desire) is beyond existence; yet the desire for this harmony that animates the work is very much in existence. One could claim that every great work is the manifestation of the futile search for God: their authenticity is in direct proportion with their inherent desire to find faith. As opposed to the Gospels, art does not affirm but asks questions; and it gains authenticity precisely because one can tell that the artist does not expect any answers whatsoever. Hopelessness does not precede (since then it could not create) or follow (since then it would propose a sort of 'positive' knowledge, in other words, answer or morale) the work, but permeates its entire structure in ways that are inseparable and indistinguishable from the work itself.

Paradoxically, a great work does not offer the experience of fulfilment by liquidating the all-pervasive impossible, but by challenging it and starting a fight despite any prospect for victory. The impossible topples the individual like Saulus was knocked down by the sight of God. It is the artist alone that attempts to fight—to be precise, those who start fighting become artists even if their fight does not culminate in an artistic form. The artist fights the impossible like Jacob fought the invisible God; but what they achieve—the work—is yet another manifestation of the impossible. The world—the artist's material—finds itself dislocated in the artwork, like Jacob's hip. As if there was an all-subverting, unbearable monster in every great work, an invisible and devastating angel. 'The tygers of wrath are wiser than the horses of instruction,' William Blake writes in *The Marriage of Heaven and Hell* (1988: 37). The horses of knowledge resign themselves to the impossible like a blind mine horse, and lose themselves never having lived the life they were granted, as opposed to the tiger that, despite having its days numbered, is not merely at the mercy of the impossible but brings the latter to life with and through its fate. 'The roaring of lions, the howling of wolves, the raging of the stormy sea, and the destructive sword, are portions of eternity too great for the eye of man,' Blake continues (ibid.: 36): everyone who challenges the impossible partakes of this 'eternity', even if it lasts for only a moment. The unutterable (the inaudible and the invisible) is the artist's true raw material; without this, there would not be anything to attach words (notes, paint or gesso) to.

It is Blake's howling of wolves that resonates in the gentlest of poems; a lion roars in the quietest music; and there is a vortex to be sensed even beyond silent paintings and motionless sculptures. Artists enjoy the impossible, although this enjoyment itself is no more than the drifting of the impossible: it cannot be distinguished from stagger-induced daze. 'The cry of shock coincides with the height of pleasure, and it is the longing sound of insurmountable loss. Prodigal nature simultaneously celebrates Saturnalia and commemorates the dead,' Nietzsche observes (1980a: 586). Artists practise this very 'cry' in order to get closer to a poetry that is universal and impersonal, in other words, to the impossible that infiltrates everything, and attempt to convey ('lay out' aided by the senses) the shock experienced in moments of divine experience in their capacity as subjects of the universe. In fact, artists would not deserve this name if their works did not radiate this sense of shock and dismay.

The God of Death

The God that emerges in such instances—as the work of art's connective tissue—could be called the God of death. In the first part of the twentieth century, magicians in Haitian death cults tried to address Death itself by calling its name. This name barely differs from the God names of Gnostic sects from two thousand years earlier. W. B. Seabrook attended such a cult and summed up his experiences as follows:

And the sexless oracle of death began to speak—if any such word as speech could be applied to the dreadful sounds that came from its throat—a series of deep, rasped gutturals, strung together on meaningless vowel monotones:

'Hgr-r-r-r-u-u-u-hgr-r-r-r-o-o-o-o-Hgr-r-r-a-a-a-a Oh-h-h-h-uu-uu-uu-uu- Bl-bl-bl—ghra-a-a- Ghu-u-u-u-u-'. It was like a prolonged death-rattle from a windpipe choked with phlegm or blood (1929: 87).

Approximately at the same time but far away from Haiti, in the midst of a radically different culture in Paris, Antonin Artaud made language explode aiming to convey the impossible colonizing his being. This was interpreted as madness by the medical profession; however, for Artaud, this constituted the very crux of existence:

main
de zolar
main
de zolan
almád
abal
main
de lupa
dabad

moioh
paiol
kirba
irba
a
didol
a bigod

It isn't written into man,
it doesn't appear in them,

what I am,
man is but a see-through matter,
that,
moves by virtue of what it is,
oppressed,
stifled
and not expressed therein,
and as a result of which, every gesture is a spontaneous
manifestation.

poiol
elti
shenets
enetis
elsid
aste

I am the infinite.
The crux of being is that I'm constantly attempting to revert
to an essence, and extort a notion, that doesn't in fact exist.
(1971: 16)

Our contemporary approach does not quite know how to handle ecstatic manifestations of death and divine experience. We tend
to talk about superstition and unenlightenment, refer to distinct
cultures as primitive, concentrate attention on the 'social' or 'psy-
chic' roots of so-called misconceptions and, in the worst case, flag
up illness or even mental illness. Our culture has been preoccupied
with stifling this experience for centuries. *Christianity* and *scientific
spirit* have deliberately attempted to excise, like surgeons, everything that could deliver the human being to the impossible. They
celebrate possibility, which in religious parlance means moral justice (the final judgement) as ultimate fulfilment, and in scientific
parlance, increasingly comprehensive knowledge and unstoppable

progress. Everything is subordinated to this, and sooner or later, one is inclined to believe that existence has a higher aim. Who would not like to believe such a thing? In moments of shock, however, when under the impact of an exceptional (be it 'uplifting' or 'distressing') experience, one loses one's footing and suddenly finds oneself in something that culture goes out of its way to deny—in the impossible—it leaves nurturing communities behind and, finding oneself on its own, loses all sense of certainty.

This uncertainty, however, is not devoid of power; yet this power is no credit to the individual. Rather, it is touched by the impossible which, moving into the human being, surpasses it like it surpasses everything else that exists. In such moments one starts to develop an affinity with those who are 'uncultured', 'primitive' or 'unenlightened', and the initiates of voodoo cults no longer appear barbarian but simply people who would not feel free without stepping into the unknown. Could death be that unknown, that Other which in particular moments places everything into the realm of the intangible? Hölderlin could hardly be labelled uncultured or unenlightened, and *Antigone* is a peak of civilization; yet, Hölderlin's writings in relation to this play on the essence of tragic representation are not addressing anything substantially different from the experience of voodoo priests, and it is not difficult to find resonances with Nietzsche's cry of shock or Blake's howling of wolves: 'Tragedy [. . .] resides in this: that the immediate God, wholly one with man [. . .] that an infinite enthusiasm infinitely, which is to say in antithesis, in consciousness that cancels out consciousness, and sacramentally departing from itself, apprehends itself, and the God, in the shape of death, is present' (Hölderlin 2001: 116).

Death permeates the moments of enthusiasm, and if one can also find the traces of God therein, then this God has not only assumed the guise of death but has also died. In other words, God can only resurrect in the human being by way of and as a result of his own death. Does this mean that one becomes 'most enthusiastic' when confronted with one's own decay, and that immersed into a timeless moment one experiences the devastating shortness of life? Could one actually prepare for death when experiencing the liveliest moments of one's life?

The Vortex of Nothingness

What is otherwise unimaginable and defies common sense becomes, in the moments of divine experience, a crushing reality and Nothing itself acquires experiential qualities. At the beginning of the sixteenth century, Charles de Bovelles writes comprehensively on the topic of Nothing in a near-forgotten and unusual treatise (*De nichilo*, 1510). The experience of Nothing must have been particularly excruciating for him, which is why he distinguished it from the logical impossibility that is non-Being:

> Every existing thing is an existing something. Everything is full of being. The void is empty, indifferent, soulless. Void is outside complete being. Consequently, the assertion 'Nothing is not nothing' has two interpretations: one of those is negative, the other is declarative and affirmative. Both reveal the same truth and are equivalent. In other words, if we state that Nothing is not nothing, or that Nothing is not non-existence, then we are saying that Nothingness is not non-existence, or if you prefer, the existing nothing is not non-existence (Bovelles 1983: 1.1).

According to Bovelles, this 'existing' Nothing can be considered the foundation for the 'existing being' (in his interpretation, of material—i.e. matter): 'Material is an unfinished and imperfect existing, potential being [. . .] material is the beginning and end of existing beings [. . .]. And the substrate of the material is nothing. Material is the basis of everything, but itself it dissolves into, rests on, nothing' (ibid.: 1.6–8). As a result, he concludes that material is neither

Being, nor non-Being, and 'is empty and free of every distinction' (ibid.: 1.9). Yet, the Nothing 'embodied' in material permeates everything that there is, since material, in his view, is both origin and end to all things. 'Nothing is the receptacle of every creature which is always present and in which they are [. . .]. Everything is therefore based on nothing: the full is in the void, being rests on non-being' (ibid.: 6.57) For Bovelles, therefore, Nothing neither surrounds existence nor 'is' beyond it, instead—anticipating Heidegger—they are inseparable though not identical. Bovelles claims that be-ing beings do not emerge and come apart from Nothing, but it is Nothing itself that permeates them after they come into being. 'Nothing does not disappear in front of creatures but co-exists with them' (ibid.), and as Hermann Broch concluded in his novel *The Death of Virgil*: 'The no thing filled the emptiness and it became the universe' (1972: 481).

The experience of Nothing allows one an insight into the fact that in order 'to be' one is also in need of the impossible, in other words, one needs that that can never exist, yet without which there would be no origin and decay.[10] Later in his work, Heidegger categorizes 'absolute Otherness' relative to existence as non-being, and likens it to Being itself:

---

10 'It is impossible rightly to utter or to say or to think of not-being without any attribute, but it is a thing inconceivable, inexpressible, unspeakable, irrational,' Plato notes in his dialogue *The Sophist* (238c). And yet, Plato subsequently concludes that the non-being, which is other than the being (*heteron*), has to exist somehow because the origin and decay of the being would be unimaginable without it:

> For we long ago gave up speaking of any opposite of being, whether it exists or not and is capable or totally incapable of definition. [. . .] The classes mingle with one another, and being and the other permeate all things, including each other, and the other, since it participates in being, is, by reason of this participation, yet is not that in which it participates, but other, and since it is other than being, must inevitably be not-being (ibid.: 258e–259a).

Being, however, is not an existing quality found in beings.
Unlike beings, being cannot be represented or brought
forth in the manner of an object. As that which is altogether other than all beings, being is that which is not. But
this nothing essentially prevails as being. [. . .] We must
prepare ourselves solely in readiness to experience in the
nothing the pervasive expanse of that which gives every
being the warrant to be. That is being itself. Without being,
whose abyssal but yet to be unfolded essence dispenses the
nothing to us in essential anxiety, all beings would remain
in an absence of being (1998c: 233).

Were we to replace the term 'Being' with God in the above quotation, we would have access to the Platonic and theological structure
of Heidegger's train of thought, and would also observe its connections to mysticism. The mystics' aim is an encounter with God
(Being), and the first step in this direction is an acceptance of
one's own Nothingness,[11] followed by the recognition that the
Nothingness of one's inner being is identical with the Nothing of
the creator.[12] Mysticism suggests that the human being experiences

---

11 As Philo of Alexandria notes: 'there was an opportunity given to the creature to approach the Creator, when he recognized his own nothingness' (*Who
Is the Heir of Divine Things* 30§).

12 A few typical examples. Tauler contends in his 45th sermon:

The soul sunken into the deepest depths of humility attracts the best
gifts of the divine abyss of love . . . The created abyss, with its boundless knowledge of its own nothingness, calleth into itself the uncreated abyss that is the infinite God, and thus is it made one with Him;
in which union the soul knows God, and yet [. . .] knows Him as
like nothing that it ever knew before; for God is nothing like the
things that man knows or can ever express (1910: 503).

Suso observes:

Essential reward [. . .] consists in the contemplative union of the
soul with the naked Godhead [. . .]. The more the soul freely goes
out of itself in detachment, the freer is its ascent; and the freer its
ascent is, the farther it enters into the wild wasteland and deep abyss
of the pathless God (1989: 243).

Nothingness when touched by God (in moments of deification); and this—despite 'Nothing'—has a clearly positive valence for mystics. Yet the experience of Nothing barely delivers fulfilment. In truth, it does not deliver emptying either, since that is a 'positive' condition, too. Much rather, it immerses the individual into a vortex that makes the two become one; and in the experience of the impossible, one experiences one's position as impossible,[13] and could only give account of it through the medium of poetry. Franz von Baader never tired of stressing that Nothing does not equal a mere zero or a sole 'indifference' but 'the highest order of difference' imaginable (1851–60: 2.102), and as such, it neither precedes existence (as prime cause, God, Being), nor follows or transcends it as fulfilment. Instead it keeps permeating it, perpetually placing it beside itself.

> People are usually [. . .] blind to the fact that the un-seen, akin to the un-heard, the un-understood, and hence the unmoved, are by no means nothing, and are not less than the seen, the heard, the perceived, the movable, but on the contrary, are more than these, since the un-seen is the seeing, the un-heard the hearing, the un-understood the understanding, and the unmoved the moving (Baader 1851–60: VOL. 4, 159–60).

Much later, yet in the same spirit, the Romantic theologian Schleiermacher noted the following:

> Observe yourself with unceasing effort. Detach all that is not yourself, always proceed with ever-sharper sense, and the more you fade from yourself, the clearer will the universe stand forth before you, the more splendidly will you be recompensed for the horror of self-annihilation through the feeling of the infinite in you (1996[1988]: 68).

13 'There is no other existent but the nothing [. . .] and all particular existence is deceptive,' Baader's contemporary and Romantic naturalist Lorenz Oken writes (1809: 11), and despite likening Nothing with God ('God is Nothing becoming self-conscious, or the existing (self-conscious) Nothing is God' [ibid.: 14]), he disputes the possibility of a final ascent.

Nothing is not an existence-transcending Being, nor is it a lack of existence, but the perpetual self-transcendence of existence. It is neither a provisional nor a final goal but a power which—as a form of Nothing—can only manifest through its own 'absence'. Therefore, one experiences Nothingness not only in fear but every time one gets energized by the impossible. Instances of wonder, pleasure, magic, joy or love can harrow us in equal ways: the more oblivious-to-oneself one might be, the higher the danger of becoming alienated from oneself. The strangeness of Being becomes one's quintessential 'essentiality'; and loaded with the 'Other', one is finally coming to one's own. When attempting to speak about this experience of Nothing, one will sooner or later fall victim to misleading words, prone to offering a running commentary on some given topic. In order to avoid sounding incomprehensible, the individual is tempted to engage in a discourse about God—the very God one witnessed in the moment of annihilation, while the latter resurrected in the human being by way of one's own death. Or else, one goes on talking about having been touched by Being—despite the fact that this experience, condensed into sensuality, is not only draining but also provides a state of saturation. Similar to God or Being, Nothingness is another guise of the impossible. In moments of the so-called divine experience, when touched by lightning, discovering the centre, crossing boundaries or ending up under the spell of chaos, one discovers one's own centre in something that lies entirely beyond one's control. This negative impression of one's self will become the sole aim of human longing, and the exclusive object of human faith in God.

CHAPTER 7

THE POWER OF NOW

Caravaggio, *Medusa*

What could human life entail if not a unique moment in which the impossible ruptures and something becomes possible? This moment between birth and death is like lightning; a luminous source that suddenly shoots off into the body of darkness. It surpasses everything while it lasts, appears indestructible and timeless, and is destroyer and creator of time. And then it disappears, just as suddenly as it came about, annihilated by the same immeasurability that led to its birth.

There would be no exceptional moments in life if life itself was not a unique and extraordinary moment of lightning. Such instances can occur at any time, since they are not connected to chronological time; they are governed by the same whimsical tyranny that ignores all sense of law and order. In moments of unsettling shock, it is this whim that permeates the individual; which is why one has the impression of having found the raw material of life, because, supposedly, that is also based on whim. Could the pointlessness of life be the utmost conclusion that one can reach? Could this be that peculiar knowledge that transpires in exceptional moments by means of the gaze, only to paralyse—akin to a Gorgon face—everything within its reach?

Time present and time past
Are both perhaps present in time future,
And time future contained in time past.

T. S. Eliot (1959: 4)

The Moment of Inspiration

In moments of inspiration, one encounters oneself as extraordinarily focused. In these remarkable moments, one believes to embark on an authentic journey through life. However, as one is coming closer to one's self, it becomes obvious that this is not happening as a result of self-effort. A peculiar power seems to be in charge. Falling in love is the condition closest to this; not for nothing do people speak of moments of rapture: while the enamoured perceives that all their yearnings are fulfilled, they simultaneously find themselves the victim of an external power which is only partially identical with the object of their desire. This unknown force will carry them away—from the world, but also from themselves. This makes moments of inspiration so haunting; as if their ultimate mission was not to impart inspiration (pleasure, rapture, suffering, doubt, love, divine experience) but to facilitate experiencing this alienation. Akin to situations when one tried to examine something from a close-up, at which point that became unrecognizable through loss of focus, when approaching fulfilment, the question of what exactly is expected to find fulfilment becomes increasingly hard to fathom.

The Sudden

It is difficult to prepare for these moments; they stalk us, catch us unawares and dissolve unannounced into Nothing, leaving only a sense of lack behind. They do not comply with any *order* or system-ization. They remain *extraordinary*. In the European Christian tra-dition, the rhythm of human life is not merely dislocated by these extraordinary occurrences, the latter also help approach the one who set their lives in motion and order: God. Intrinsically linked to this is the story of Saul's similarly instant conversion:

> As he journeyed he came near Damascus, and suddenly a light shone around him from heaven. Then he fell to the ground, and heard a voice saying to him, 'Saul, Saul, why are you persecuting Me?' And he said, 'Who are You, Lord?' Then the Lord said, 'I am Jesus, whom you are persecuting. It is hard for you to kick against the goads.' [. . .] And the men who journeyed with him stood speechless, hearing a voice but seeing no one. Then Saul arose from the ground, and when his eyes were opened he saw no one. But they led him by the hand and brought him into Damascus. And he was three days without sight, and neither ate nor drank (Apostles 9:3–9).

Allegedly, God is awaiting Saul at the end of this road. And yet, there is no trace of peace in this encounter. His fall divests Saul of his self, as Caravaggio's painting *The Conversion of Saint Paul* skil-fully illustrates. The Lord cautions Saul that not even his instinct, the supposedly most private component of his being, belongs to him: this too is under his command. Naturally, Paul will subse-quently interpret this moment of 'great suddenness' as an obvious fulfilment. Yet there and then, instead of fulfilment, the confusion is profuse: regarding both height and depth (falling to the ground) as well as light and dark (turning blind). The aftermath of this moment surpasses order (this main characteristic of God) as well as its opposite: disorder. This is reminiscent of chaos, wherefrom the human being has always attempted to keep away, and what one tries to dissimulate at all costs by aiming to decipher the seal of divine grace. What is this 'great suddenness'? The original Greek expression betrays its meaning. To denote 'sudden', the Greek text uses the word *exaiphnes*, and it is not for the first time that this word assumes a major role. Plato uses it in a different, equally remarkable context. Plato's dialogue *Parmenides* about the relation between Oneness and Being explains that calmness and motion, origin and decay cannot happen simultaneously: 'It is impossible for it to be previously at rest and afterwards in motion, or previously in motion and afterwards at rest' (*Parmenides* 156c). But then where should the transformation take place, whereby the previous state has not yet been overcome and the subsequent one has not been reached? Socrates suggests the instantaneous and the sudden (*to exaiphnes*):

> This strange instantaneous nature [*physis atopos* = not location-bound], something interposed between motion and rest, not existing in any time, and into this and out from this that which is in motion changes into rest and that which is at rest changes into motion [. . .]. Then the one, if it is at rest and in motion, must change in each direction; for that is the only way in which it can do both. But in changing, it changes instantaneously, and when it changes *it can be in no time*, and at that instant it will be neither in motion nor at rest. [. . .] And will the case not be the same in relation to other changes? When it changes from being to destruction or from not being to becoming, does it not pass into an intermediate stage between certain forms of motion and rest, so that it neither is nor is not, neither comes into being nor is destroyed? (ibid., 156d–157a, emphasis added).

Kierkegaard calls the Platonic concept of the 'instantaneous' a 'category of transition' (1980: 81): while it makes it possible for the now to connect to a later now, its role is not limited to mere mediation. The instantaneous does not benefit from being approached from the dimensions of time or space, since the latter originate by way of its contribution. In fact, the instantaneous is akin to an unpaired hyphen. Just as order is a tiny, demarcated slice of the exceptional, so too is time embedded in something chronologically incommensurable.[1] For the duration of the jolt that constitutes the instantaneous, Nothing occurs—to be precise, 'Nothing' reveals itself, because it allows for something to happen that cannot be enclosed into a spatial or chronological dimension. In these extraordinary moments, it becomes obvious that space and time are not an ultimate anchor but merely a veil. Moments like this also reveal that this veil—similar to the veil of Sais—does not conceal anything. Nothing hides behind it, or, to be clearer, it is 'Nothing' that yet again is to be found behind it. In these extraordinary instances, it is not the curtain of space or time that is lifted for Nothing, so that we can contemplate it like a spectacle from the auditorium of our world, but it is Nothing, impossibility itself that handles the curtain, thus doing away with the difference between stage (distant transcendence) and audience (sense-world). This makes us simultaneously spectators and embodiment of this impossible, which lurks everywhere and breaks forth in such extraordinary moments. Life's connective tissue is thus being revealed, although it is no less remarkable that we are spared its continuous perception.

'Enlightenment'

Plato considered the sudden 'something strange', using the word *atopos*, originally understood as 'not in its place'. In the 'all-of-the-sudden', that which has no special dimension enters space, without thus joining the space and time continuum.[2] It is this 'strangeness'

---

1 Aristotle attempted to reject this ever-present paradox when he subjected what he called the 'sudden', that is the exceptional, to time and order: 'The sudden is what is displaced in a time imperceptible on account of smallness' (*Physics* 4.222b; Sachs 2004 trans.) [Earlier translations of Aristotle use the term 'presently' to convey this notion of the instantaneous or sudden, see Hippocrates G. Apostle's translation (Aristotle 1969).—Trans.]

2 Aristotle did not only attempt to subject the 'sudden' to time but also denied the possibility of spacelessness: 'The place and the body cannot but fit each other. Neither is the whole place larger than what can be filled by the body (and then

that makes itself being felt in moments of inspiration. Such moments are unplannable and unpredictable. They are unsuitable as a basis for institutions required towards the operation of societal life; which is why, looking back on them from the perspective of time and order, humans try to downgrade the importance of these moments. Indicative of this is that in the New Testament, the attribute *atopos* is no longer used to express something miraculous, but morally reprehensible events: something 'amiss' (Luke 23:41), harm (Apostles 28:6), unreasonable and wicked (2 Thessalonians 3:2). For Plato, the instantaneous (*exaiphnes*) was still connected to the miraculous (*atopos*), that is with the impossible that transcends origin and decay. For Christians, these exclude each other. The sudden (the moment of Saul's conversion) is the expression of an unambiguous, positively conceived grace, which is nevertheless placeless (*atopos*), protruding from divine order and, therefore, must embody evil. What initially was both ravishing and destructive, uplifting and paralysing, with the expansion of Christianity has became experienced as bifurcation. This division suggests an image of God presumed to be comprehensible, harmonious and accessible. Even 'faith in divine grace' rests on the conviction that the human being can never exercise complete command over its fate. Instead of confronting this paradox and taking account of the possibility of finding 'fulfilment' in the impossible—which ultimately challenges this very fulfilment, this faith domesticates the paradox to a resolvable contradiction and likens fulfilment with the reconciliation of opposites.

Truth be told, Christianity had not become completely unfaithful to Plato. In *Parmenides*, the instantaneous can still free humans

---

the body would no longer be infinite), nor is the body larger than the place; for either there would be an empty space or a body whose nature it is to be nowhere' (*Physics* 3.205a–b, Hardie and Gaye 2006 trans). Aristotle does not consider the impossible (endowed with the most potential) as the ultimate foundation, but locates order, in other words, the perceptible and controllable as the ultimate criteria of existence.

from the captivity of time and circumstances, because one cannot be reduced to either origin or decay. In his letters, however, Plato recontextualizes the terms 'instantaneous' and 'sudden'. The final discovery, he writes, 'does not at all admit of verbal expression like other studies, but, as a result of continued application to the subject itself and communion therewith, it is brought to birth in the soul on a sudden, as light that is kindled by a leaping spark, and thereafter it nourishes itself' (*Epistles* 341c–d). The 'sudden' is unperceptively subordinated to something else. This does not consist of a 'miraculous' (non-place-bound) knowledge any more but of 'something final'—which is no longer reminiscent of the rule of the impossible but of 'communal effort' and 'true communal life'—that is to say, of strictly time-based circumstances. The instantaneous has no longer the task of acting as an independent yet 'transitional' category, which condenses duration into a singular, vertiginous instant, but has become a bridgehead to what could be described as harmonious divine eternity. The concepts of the instantaneous and sudden (*exaiphnés*) are later used by Plotinus to convey divine enlightenment: the ascending human being 'beholds [. . .] Oneness in pan/synoptic conjunction' (*exaiphnés*) (*Enneads* 6.7.36) in order for light to pour into its eye and sight. Here too, ecstatic convulsion is subject to something else, and is meant to serve the intellect and rational insight. Just how unencumbered this wish could infiltrate Christian culture and mysticism can be exemplified by one of Dionysius the Areopagite's fifth-century observations. He did not experience in the moment the miracle of the subversive impossible but witnessed an occurrence of transubstantiation:

> 'Sudden' is that which, contrary to expectation, and out of the, as yet, unmanifest, is brought into the manifest. But with regard of Christ's love of man, I think that the Word of God suggests even this that the Superessential proceeded forth out of the hidden, into the manifestation amongst us, by having taken substance as man. But, He is hidden, even after the manifestation, or to speak more divinely, even in

the manifestation, for in truth this of Jesus has been kept hidden, and the mystery with respect to Him has been reached by no word nor mind, but even when spoken, remains unsaid, and when conceived unknown (1897: 142).

God is unspeakable and unrecognizable not by dint of the distance the human individual would have to cover in order to rise up to him, but by being so close to what one calls 'God'. To utilize Meister Eckhart's phrase: 'God is closer to me than I to myself' (quoted in Mahnke 1937: 72). This implies that, in profoundly poignant moments, one is less troubled by God's magnitude and might than by one's own declining self-identity. More than ever before, one is under the impression of having achieved a rapprochement with one's very nature—but one's identity manifests itself in utter and insurmountable non-identity. This non-identity is blinding (see Saul!) to such an extent that one can no longer gauge what one has drawn near or moved away from.

The Absence of Existence

Every instance of knowledge and sight is directed towards something specific; knowledge requires an object just as much as seeing, and in order to approach an object, coordination is paramount. Aristotle claims, however, that the movement of the soul and of the object is none other than time itself, since existence always spreads out in time. *When time ruptures in the here and now, as a result of the sudden, existence itself experiences an unfillable void.* A sense of timelessness takes over the human being, as if Nothing would start to diffuse around it. Nothing is but a negation and absence of existence. Since existence is gapless, the sense of lack that one experiences in profoundly poignant moments does not signify the negation of one be-ing being by another (comparable to the displacement of one body by another) but, rather, the appearance of something that is responsible for the cycle of genesis and decay, something which neither originates nor decays, so, strictly speaking, does not exist at all.

One can investigate how things are, yet one cannot decipher why they exist. In order to do this, it would be necessary to prescind from their existence, and to search for an explanation where it is the least possible: in their absence and non-existence. Everything that exists, is saturated with what exists 'beyond' existence, which therefore is inappropriately labelled as 'something'. This is that, that was not, and will not be, but is, while it really is not. Parmenides describes this IS by saying that it has never been, and will never be, yet it is now, continuously as a unique whole (DK 28B8, 5–6). As Boethius later cautions us, the use of this IS is only permitted if we do not understand it as a verbal tense but as a timeless presence that can only be interpreted as the present of revelation.[3] But even the use of this timeless IS does not suffice to render that this IS is pregnant with NOT IS. Therefore, it is fundamentally impossible to say that it IS or that it IS NOT; that it is BEING or that it is NOTHING; that it is THIS or NOT THIS. To put it differently, this is none other than the eternal IMPOSSIBLE.

The Feud between Time and Eternity

Time is a prison, declared the Gnostics; a sign of the banishment from completeness and the perfection of the Pleroma (see Schultz 1986: 35). They believed that evil pervades by means of time (Cosmocrator = Chromocrator), and therefore considered escaping from time's rule as a precondition for the liberation from the

3 Boethius contends:

> For we shall not allow anyone to say that the knowledge of the gods runs along with the flow of things, nor that anything with them is past or future. Nor shall we allow that 'was' and 'will be' are used among them, words which, as we have heard from Plato's Timaeus, signify some change. Only 'is' is used, and that not the 'is' which is counted in with 'was' and 'will be' and contrasted with them, but the 'is' which is conceived before the level of temporal images, and which signifies the gods' undeviating unchangeability. This is the 'is' which the great Parmenides also says belongs to all that is unthinkable, when he says 'for it was not, nor will it be. All together, it is alone' (quoted in Sorabji 1983: 102).

dominion of evil. In this, we can trace an earlier concept, the Persian distinction between time and eternity, *zrvan dareghō chvad-hātá* and *zrvam akarná*. According to this view, universal time (that is the time from creation to the end of the world) and boundless time (eternity) are opposite each other. This thought re-emerges in Plato's history of creation, too, in *Timaeus*:

> He set about making this Universe, so far as He could, of a like kind. But inasmuch as the nature of the Living Creature was eternal, this quality was impossible to attach in its entirety to what is generated; wherefore He planned to make a movable image of Eternity, and, as He set in order the Heaven, of that Eternity which abides in unity He made an eternal image, moving according to number, even that which we have named Time. For simultaneously with the construction of the Heaven He contrived the production of days and nights and months and years, which existed not before the Heaven came into being. And these are all portions of Time; even as 'Was' and 'Shall be' are generated forms of Time, although we apply them wrongly, without noticing, to Eternal Being. For we say that it 'is' or 'was' or 'will be', whereas, in truth of speech, 'is' alone (37d–e).

Though this distinction between time and supra-temporality is appropriate, these terms cannot be opposed in the manner of harmonious heavenly silence versus earthly conflict. Everything that exists is subject to the perpetually moving state between genesis and decay; and yet, existence does not only provoke the idea of everlasting change but also of immutablilty. As the Neoplatonic Damascius contends: every single point of a river is in constant flux, yet everything in between its source and mouth constitutes a single and lasting whole (quoted in Simplicius, *Physics*, 774.35). This holds true for all things in the process of becoming and perishing. They were and will be, that is to say, they are subject to time, while they also surpass time by dint of their sheer existence. *The supposedly timeless is neither faraway nor divine but the continuously self-erasing*

*raw material of life; and earthly time is not a movement taking place
away from eternity but a function of its overflowing effervescence.*
When the eternity-craving human being finds itself torn out of
time, one does not simply step into the eternal but, rather, experiences that the eternal does not exist 'beyond' but 'within' time. Time
is not 'eclipsed' by eternity, but—akin to be-ing beings in relation
to non-be-ing beings—actually transcends the latter. Both are
dependent on, and superior to each other, and both operate as each
other's ultimate lack and fulfilment.

Ever since Neoplatonism and early Christianity, it has become
customary to identify the Eternal (the One, God) with an extensionless now, and to contrast this with time itself.[4] In parallel, the
idea of an irresolvable conflict is also being supplanted—naturally,
since those 'in support of' conflict do not see the eternal as fulfilment but as the destructive raw material of temporal life. They perceive the eternal as divested of its own self and frustrating any of
hope for change. The early Gnostics cautioned against unavoidable

---

4 A precondition of this was distinguishing between endless time, timelessness
(*sempiternitas*) and eternity (*aeternitas*, by definition excluding a sense of time).
Boethius contends:

> But the 'is always' (*semper*) which is said of God signifies a single idea,
> as if he has been there in all the past, is there in some way in all the
> present, and will be there in all the future. According to philosophers,
> the same can be said about the heavens and the other deathless bodies,
> but it is not said of God in the same way. For he is always because
> 'always' in him belongs to the present, and there is a great difference
> between the present of our affairs, which is now, and the present of
> divine matters. For our now, as if running, creates time and sempiternity
> (*sempiternitas*), whereas the divine now stays not moving, but standing
> still, and creates eternity (*aeternitas*) (quoted in ibid.: 116).

More than a millennium later, Bovelles divides time as follows in his treatise on
Nothing: *aeternitas* (a limitless period without beginning and end), *aevum* (has a
beginning, but no end—according to Bonaventura this created eternity [*aeviterni-
tas*] characterizes matter—see Jehl 1984: 23), *tempus* (a period with beginning and
end—time proper) and *instans* (an impulse likened to a dot, without expanse—
momentum) (1983: Chap. 2).

conflict, denying the chance for reconciliation between temporal life and the eternal. Despite envisioning final and eternal peace, mystics are bound to fall into the pitfall of paradoxes so that they are silenced by means of the eternal No in lieu of absolution. Baader considers time the suspension of the eternal, and hence argues that one 'does not reach eternity by taking no notice of or prescinding from time, but by catching a glimpse of it by way of immersion therein' (Baader 1851–60: VOL. 7, 372); Blake notes in 'The Proverbs of Hell': 'Eternity is in love with the productions of time' (1988: 36); Kierkegaard, whose favourite concept was the moment, writes on the paradoxical manifestation of eternity: 'The moment is that ambiguity in which time and eternity touch each other, and with this the concept of *temporality* is posited, whereby time constantly intersects eternity and eternity constantly pervades time' (1980: 89); Nietzsche considered preoccupation with the moment a condition of authentic life, despite these 'divine moments' not being the harbingers of happiness: 'Once I yearned for happy signs from birds; then you led an owl abomination across my path, a repulsive one. Alas, where then did my tender yearning flee?' (Nietzsche 2006: 86); or Bataille, who advocated self-immersion into sovereign moments which can instil a sympathy for death. Profoundly poignant moments are not only crushing by virtue of the existence of a pre-sumed God but in conjunction with the heightened awareness of one's own mortality. The eternity of the impossible and its timeless 'now' stands opposed to another aspect of the timeless moment: while endowed with the gift of life, the individual also feels short-changed, a feeling for which mortality is the most eloquent proof.

Presence

In extraordinary moments, it is not the experience of this or that concrete matter that becomes intense, but, rather, it is destructive intensity that begins to fill the human being up. John Keats analysed in his famous odes the relationship between the moment and eternity as well as the question whether the time-trapped individual can experience a sense of completeness. Keats' answer is definitively affirmative. For him, moments of wholeness constitute life's greatest achievement. Keats does not entertain illusions, however. These moments might be the most intense in life, but this intensity is not a function exclusive to wholeness, as it also appears in connection to death.[5] In his poem *Endymion*, Keats portrays the achievement of a sense of wholeness as a 'self-destructive' process which will nevertheless lead to an 'utmost intensity' (1973a: 1.799–800). In 'Why Did I Laugh Tonight?', one of his most enigmatic sonnets, death signifies the state of highest intensity, which does not exclude life but, on the contrary, stands as its most cherished gift: 'Verse, Fame, and Beauty are intense indeed, / But Death intenser—Death is Life's high meed' (1973b: 328).

In this context, intensity can be best described as presence. There is no intensity without power, and no power without efficiency, since the efficient is always present. The Latin word *praesens* (present) does

---

5 Ever since the age of Romanticism, when the idea of God's death first emerged, intensity has also become synonymous with the abandonment of mankind—which, as long as it is not related to a supposed God, does not connote despoilment but positive completeness. This is why Bataille considers intensity as the utmost value:

> If the sensations do not have their greatest intensity, it is possible for us to isolate specific objects on the field of the totality; whereupon we no longer know anything but those objects; we know them clearly and distinctly, but the presence of the totality escapes us. The sense of the totality demands an extreme intensity of *the vaguest sensations, which reveal to us nothing clear or distinct*: these are essentially animal sensations, which are not merely rudimentary, which bring back our animality, effecting the reversal without which we could not reach the totality. Their high-pitched intensity overruns us, and they suffocate us at the very moment they overthrow us morally. The negation of nature (of animality) is what separates us from the concrete totality: it inserts us in the abstractions of a human order—where, like so many artful fairies, work, science and bureaucracy change us into abstract entities. But the embrace restores us, not to nature (which is itself, if it is not reintegrated, only a detached part), but rather to the totality in which man has his share by *losing himself* (1987: 269).

not only refer to the present tense but also to the power of gods. The word signifies poison as well (one of the most coercive pieces of evidence that can be provided for effective presence!), and originally derived from 'roundabout' before its meaning was 'restricted' to the power and presence of gods.[6] In Antiquity, one only referred to presence in connection to gods and heroes, since presence is super-human. It confers the feeling of being divine; as soon as we experi-ence our own one-off presence, we are being released from the shackles of circumstances. Maps, compasses and milestones merely reveal where one is, and not whether one is present or not. Presence is not a physically determined state. On the contrary, it is a radiating aura, which, akin to a winning glance or smile, is capable of con-juring up a spherically enclosed world.

If one is lost to time, then one spends little time in the present. One relies on the future and feeds on the past, attributing no sig-nificance to the moment of 'now'. 'Now' is perceived as something intangible, a logical impossibility, and one finds existence inconceiv-able seeing that as soon as its name is uttered, it already belongs to the realm of the past.[7] Thus, these extraordinary moments testify that what the individual used to think impossible, is possible indeed, and 'now' itself gains independence. These are life's most intense

---

6 'Their choir asks for help, and feels the divine presence. (*Praesentia numina sentit*.)' (Horace, *Epistles* 2.1.134, translation modified).

7 The 'now' that Parmenides mentions in relation to THERE IS does not form part of time and, therefore, one cannot claim that it is endowed with content: it surpasses time altogether. It is not identical with the now that tends to be referred to as the smallest unit of time, and is perceived by some as 'time atom' (Epicure writes about atoms that cannot be further divided [*Letter to Herodotus* 47.62], as does Lucretius [*On the Nature of Things* 4.794–6]), as time limit by others (according to Bovelles, the moment = *temporis extremum* [1983: Chap. 2]), and by yet others the intangible (Aristotle talks about the Nothingness of 'now' [*Physics* 4.218a], followed by St Augustine [*Confessions* 11.16, 27] and Hegel [1951: 88]). THERE IS cannot be con-nected to a particular tense—be it present, future or past, since all of these are made possible through it, and similarly the term 'now' used in conjunction with it is but a metaphorical description of what cannot in fact be described.

moments. Presence grows into an inner force enabling the individual to step out of oneself, as space and time merge spasmodically. These moments of presence convince the individual that while one lives in the present, life is nevertheless not solely time-based: it is being sustained by the eternity of the 'now-and-never-again'. One recognizes that each and every moment is equidistant from 'God'; each is unique and exceptional. In these special moments, one is touched by what remains the same in all moments past and future, and what, therefore, surpasses them all: the present unrestricted in time.

The Fear of the Immeasurable

Living within the confines of time has an instinctively soothing effect on the individual; one surrenders to duration, which does not reassure by dint of its length but of its actual span. However, in extraordinary moments it becomes obvious that duration, often understood as life's natural riverbed, is a wall, too. It is a separating wall that keeps one away from what is best not taken notice of.

If time and duration are instances of measure, then the revealing moment is none other than excess. This illustrates that it is not time that gives birth to the moment.[8] On the contrary, time is a manifestation of the force which inhabits everything that is, and of which the moment is the most obvious expression. Everything that there is is measurable, if by no other means then by being given a name of some sort. But what creates life is unnameable, since language itself is only one of the things that exist. In the same way as the moment brings forth time, this unnameable brings forth—and dispossesses—all that exists.

---

8 Akin to numerous forerunners and followers, Adelard of Bath thought in the first part of the twelfth century that 'time consists of the following: years, months, hours, minutes, points, moments and instants. [. . .] Instants (*instans*) form a part of time, yet they cannot be subdivided into further sections. Moments also form part of time, and are made up of 572 instants' (quoted in Ritter and Gründer 1971–84: VOL. 6, 100).

This thought is no stranger to mystics, such as Dionysius the Areopagite or his enthusiastic exegete from the ninth century, Scotus Erigena. And yet, when facing the ultimate immeasurable, the impossible, even they seem to recoil in the last moment, and label the unnameable 'God'. The respectful awe for measure—or much rather, for the fear of excess—gains the upper hand in them. This unacknowledged anxiety explains why extraordinary moments are so often denounced, and at times denied altogether. A society or a community can only be founded on a shared belief in measure, and they could not operate unless they were set up for the long haul. This renders the rule of the moment, of the here and now, dangerous, as it demonstrates that society is not the ultimate criterion for human existence. Every duration is finite, even infinitesimally short if observed from the death-dealing perspective of the timeless moment. In extraordinary moments, it becomes obvious that there is no society to alleviate the burden of the fleetingness of human existence, and that one cannot rely on others in the end. The world of measure and duration helps the human being to stay well grounded, but its eventual failure proves none other than the fact that one is constantly being stalked by predatory immeasurability and timelessness. This is what all cultures attempt to hide, and—by way of naming and attaching labels—what religions are trying to conceal.

The Burden of Mortality

What else could constitute human life but a unique moment in which the impossible ruptures and something becomes possible? The moment between birth and death resembles a flash of lightning: a luminous source that suddenly shoots off into the body of darkness. It surpasses everything while it lasts, appears indestructible and timeless, and it is destroyer and creator of time alike. And then it disappears, just as suddenly as it came about, annihilated by the same immeasurability that led to its birth.

There would be no extraordinary moments if life itself was not a unique, exceptional and momentary flash of light that could come about on any occasion. It is not bound to time, and is led with moody arbitrariness by the vortex that ignores all signs of law and order. It is this whimsicality that overwhelms the individual in profoundly poignant moments, and one is led to the belief of having encountered the essence of life because arbitrariness seems to be at the core of the latter, too. Yet what if one's realization that life is gratuitous were to be the only insight to be gained? Thus, one finds it hard to comprehend why one happens to live at the time when one does, neither earlier nor later, and why one was born in the first place. One was given life without having asked for it, and will see this life being taken back, yet again without one's consent. These extraordinary moments reveal life's completely random nature, as well as the enviable absence of a legion of beings who have never got the chance to be conceived. In such situations, one longs for the company of the unborn; this appears as the one and only prospect for bypassing this perverse eternity called death.

Held Captive in the Moment

Could eternal time be contained in this infinitely tiny speck that is human life? And could the vastness of space gain its infinity by way of the human body? Does not one experience fulfilment when losing oneself while encountering the all-consuming impossible? Is not one overwhelmed by a sense of achievement in the very moments of trauma? Is not it then that one learns that there is no greater treasure than the intensity of the extensionless moment? Does not one only start to truly live in the face of threat, extinction and dismay at preordained human decay? Is not the yearning for being alive the greatest when the danger of death is most imminent? And anyway, is there anything left to crave in these moments? Does not one simply harken to the ever-accelerating rhythm of one's very own heartbeat?

WORKS CITED

The Acts of John. 1983[1924]. In *The Apocryphal New Testament* (Montague Rhodes James trans.). Oxford: Clarendon, pp. 228–69.

AELIANUS. 1958–59. *On the Characteristics of Animals* (A. F. Scholfield trans.). Loeb Classical Library. Cambridge, MA: Harvard University Press.

AESCHYLUS. 1926. *The Libation Bearers* (Herbert Weir Smyth trans.). Cambridge, MA: Harvard University Press.

ALBRIGHT, W. F. 1957. *From the Stone Age to Christianity*. New York: Doubleday.

APOLLODORUS. 1921. *The Library* (J. G. Frazer trans.). Loeb Classical Library. Cambridge, MA: Harvard University Press.

AQUINAS, Thomas. 2007. *Summa Theologica*, VOL. 1, PART 1 (Fathers of the English Dominican Province trans.). New York: Cosimo Classics.

ARISTOTLE. 1969. *Aristotle's Physics* (Hippocrates G. Apostle trans.). Bloomington: Indiana University Press.

——. 2004. *Aristotle's Physics: A Guided Study* (Joe Sachs trans.). New Brunswick and London: Rutgers University Press.

——. 2006. *Physics* (R. P. Hardie and R. K. Gaye trans). Adelaide: University of Adelaide Library.

ARTAUD, Antonin. 1965. *Anthology* (Jack Hirschman ed.). San Francisco: City Lights Books.

——. 1971. 'Notes pour une "Lettre aux Balinais"'. *Tel Quel* 46: 10–34.

AUGUSTINE. 1943. *Confessions* (J. G. Pilkington trans.). New York: Liveright.

BAADER, Franz von. 1851–60. *Sämmtliche Werke*, 15 VOLS. Leipzig: Verlag des Literarischen Instituts.

Baal and Anath. n.d. Simon B. Parker (trans.). Available at: http://bit.ly/-31VOnzL (last accessed on 12 January 2020).

BALTHASAR, Hans Urs von. 1969. 'Mysterium Paschale' in *Mysterium Salutis. Grundriß heilsgeschichtlicher Dogmatik*, PART 3, VOL. 2: *Das Christusereignis* (Johannes Feiner and Magnus Löhrer eds). Einsiedeln: Benziger, pp. 133–326.

BATAILLE, Georges. 1988. *Guilty* (Bruce Boone trans.). Venice, CA: Lapis Press.

———. 1997. *The Bataille Reader* (Fred Botting and Scott Wilson eds). Oxford: Blackwell.

BERGFLETH, Gerd. 1987. 'Beethoven-Dionysos' in *Der Pfahl*, VOL. 1. Munich: Matthes und Seitz.

The Bhagavad Gita. n.d. Shri Purohit Swami (trans.). Available at: http://bit.ly/2tZbD3g (last accessed on 12 January 2020).

The Bible. New Revised Standard Version. Available at: http://bit.ly/2SKmZR8 (last accessed on 12 January 2020).

BLAKE, William. 1988. *The Complete Poetry and Prose* (David V. Erdman ed.). New York: Doubleday.

BÖHME, Jacob. 1910. *The Three Principles of the Divine Essence* (John Sparrow trans.). London: John M. Watkins. Available at: http://bit.ly/2WsXZP6 (last accessed on 4 May 2019).

———. 2010. *Mysterium Magnum: An Exposition of the First Book of Moses Called Genesis* (John Sparrow trans.). Available at: https://goo.gl/oaJJbm (last accessed on 7 July 2018).

———. 2019. *The Clavis, or An Explanation of Some Principal Points and Expressions*. Available at: http://bit.ly/2V1MEnw (last accessed on 4 May 2019).

BONAVENTURE. 1885. *Opera Omnia ad Clarus Aquas (Quaracchi)*, VOL. 3: *Commentaria in Quatuor Libres Sententiarum Magistri Pétri Lombardi*. Florence: Collegio s. Bonaventura.

The Book of the Dead, or Going Forth by Day. 1974. Chicago: Oriental Institute of the University of Chicago.

The Books of Jeu, and the Untitled Text in the Bruce Codex. 1978. Carl Schmidt (ed.), Violet Macdermot (trans.). Leiden: E. J. Brill.

BOVELLES, Charles de. 1983. *Le livre du néant* (P. Magnard trans.). Paris: Lib - raire Philosophique J. Vrin.

BRECHT, Martin. 1981. *Martin Luther. Sein Weg zur Reformation, 1483–1531*. Stuttgart: Calwer Verlag.

BROCH, Hermann. 1972. *The Death of Virgil* (Jean Starr Untermeyer trans.). New York: Vintage International.

BROWNE, Thomas. 1964a. *Pseudodoxia Epidemica* in *The Works of Sir Thomas Browne* (Geoffrey Keynes ed.), VOL. 2. London: Faber and Faber.

———. 1964b. *Religio Medici* in *The Works of Sir Thomas Browne*, VOL. 1. London: Faber and Faber, pp. 1–90.

CAGE, John. 1973. 'Lecture on Nothing' (1949) in *Silence: Lectures and Writings*. Middletown, CT: Wesleyan University Press, pp. 109–27.

CÉLINE, Louis-Ferdinand. 2003. *The Church: A Comedy in Five Acts* (Mark Spitzer and Simon Green trans). Los Angeles: Green Integer Books.

DELCOURTE, Marie. 1955. *L'Oracle de* Delphes. Paris: Payot.

DIELS, Hermann Alexander. 1952. *Die Fragmente der Vorsokratiker*, 6th EDN (Walther Kranz revd), 3 VOLS. Berlin: Weidmann.

DIONYSIUS THE AREOPAGITE. 1897. *The Works of Dionysius the Areopagite* (John Parker trans.). London: James Parker & Company.

ECKHART, Meister. 1909. *Meister Eckhart's Sermons* (Claude Field trans.). London: H. R. Allenson.

ELIADE, Mircea. 1958. *Yoga: Immortality and Freedom* (Willard R. Trask trans.). London: Arkana.

———. 1969. *Le myth de l'éternel retour*. Paris: Gallimard.

———. 1978. *Die Religionen und das Heilige*. Darmstadt: Wissenschaftliche Buchgesellschaft.

ELIOT, T. S. 1959. *Four Quartets*. London: Faber and Faber.

ERIGENA, Scotus. 1987. *Periphyseon: The Division of Nature* (I. P. Sheldon-Williams trans., John J. O'Meara revd). Montreal: Bellarmin.

EURIPIDES. 1906. *The Bacchae* (Gilbert Murray trans.), 2nd EDN. London: George Allen.

———. 1937. *Ion* (H. D. trans.). London: Chatto and Windus.

EUSEBIUS OF CAESAREA. 1903. *Praeparatio Evangelica* (E. H. Gifford trans.). Available at: https://goo.gl/rtNu7V (last accessed on 26 May 2017).

FRAZER, James. 1963. *The Golden Bough, Part Four: Adonis, Attis, Osiris*. London: Macmillan.

FREEMAN, Kathleen. 1983[1948]. *Ancilla to the Pre-Socratic Philosophers*. Cambridge, MA: Harvard University Press.

GOETHE, Johann Wolfgang von. 1908. *Poetry and Truth from My Own Life* (Minna Steele Smith trans.). London: George Bell.

GOSSE, Philip Henry. 1857. *Omphalos: An Attempt to Untie the Geological Knot*, London: John Van Voorst.

GRABBE, Christian Dietrich. 1963. *Don Juan and Faust* (Maurice Edwards trans.) in Oscar Mandel (ed.), *The Theatre of Don Juan: A Collection of Plays and Views, 1630–1963*. Lincoln: University of Nebraska Press, pp. 331–97.

HARRISON, Jane. 1957. *Prolegomena to the Study of Greek Religion*. New York: Meridian Books.

———. 1962. *Epilegomena to the Study of Greek Religion and Themis*. New York: University Books.

HEGEL, G. W. F. 1951. *Phänomenologie des Geistes* in *Sämtliche Werke*, VOL. 2 (Hermann Glockner ed.). Stuttgart: Fr. Frommanns Verlag.

———. 1961. 'The Spirit of Christianity and Its Fate' in *On Christianity: Early Theological Writings of Friedrich Hegel* (T. M. Knox trans., Richard Kroner introd.). New York: Harper Torchbooks, pp. 182–301.

———. 1971. 'The Spirit of Christianity and Its Fate' in *Early Theological Writings* (T. M. Knox trans., Richard Kroner introd. and fragments trans.). Philadelphia: University of Pennsylvania Press, pp. 182–301.

HEIDEGGER, Martin. 1954. *Vorträge und Aufsätze*. Pfullingen: Günther Neske.

———. 1957. *Der Satz vom Grund*. Pfullingen: Neske.

———. 1978. *Vom Wesen und Begriff der Physis. Aristoteles, Physik B1*. Frankfurt am Main: Vittorio Klostermann.

———. 1998a. 'On the Essence and Concept of Physis in Aristotle's Physics B, I' (Thomas Sheehan trans.) in *Pathmarks* (William McNeill ed.). Cambridge: Cambridge University Press, pp. 183–230.

———. 1998b. 'Plato's Doctrine of Truth' (Thomas Sheehan trans.) in *Pathmarks* (William McNeill ed.). Cambridge: Cambridge University Press, pp. 155–82.

———. 1998c. 'Postscript to "What Is Metaphysics?"' (William McNeill trans.) in *Pathmarks* (William McNeill ed.). Cambridge: Cambridge University Press, pp. 231–8.

———. 1998d. 'What Is Metaphysics?' (David Farrell Krell trans.) in *Pathmarks* (William McNeill ed.). Cambridge: Cambridge University Press, pp. 82–96.

HESIOD. 1914. *Theogony* (H. G. Evelyn-White trans.) in *Homeric Hymns, Epic Cycle, Homerica*. Loeb Classical Library. Cambridge, MA: Harvard University Press.

HOMER. 1898. *Iliad* (Samuel Butler trans.). London: Longmans, Green.

——. 1919. *The Odyssey* (A. T. Murray trans.). Loeb Classical Library. Cambridge, MA: Harvard University Press.

HÖLDERLIN, Friedrich. 1952. *Sämtliche Werke*, VOL. 5. Stuttgart: W. Kohlhammer Verlag.

——. 2001. 'Hölderlin's Notes to *Antigone*' in *Hölderlin's Sophocles: Oedipus and Antigone* (David Constantine ed. and trans.). Newcastle: Bloodaxe Books.

——. 2004. 'Bread and Wine' in *The Poems of Hölderlin* (James Mitchell comp. and trans.). San Francisco: Ithuriel's Spear, pp. 7–15.

——. 2007. 'Patmos' in *Poems of Friedrich Hölderlin* (James Mitchell ed. and trans.). San Francisco, CA: Ithuriel's Spear, pp. 39–45.

HORACE. 1926. *Satires. Epistles. The Art of Poetry* (H. Rushton Fairclough trans.). Loeb Classical Library. Cambridge, MA: Harvard University Press.

HYPPOLITUS. n.d. *Against All Heresies*. Available at: http://bit.ly/2OQmLqv (last accessed on 19 May 2017).

IPOLYI, Arnold. 1854. *Magyar mythologia*. Pest: Heckenast.

IRENAEUS OF LYONS. n.d. *Against Heresies*. Available at: https://goo.gl/5eE3hy (last accessed on 8 September 2016).

JEHL, Rainer. 1984. *Melancholie und Acedia. Ein Beitrag zu Anthropologie und Ethik Bonaven-turas*, Paderborn: Schöningh Verlag.

JENNI, Ernst, and Claus Westermann. 1976. *Theologisches Handwörterbuch zum Alten Testament*. Munich: Kaiser Verlag.

JOYCE, James. 1986[1922]. *Ulysses*. New York: Random House.

JUNG, Carl Gustav. 1970. *Aion: Researches into the Phenomenology of the Self* (R. F. C. Hull trans.). Princeton, NJ: Princeton University Press.

KAFKA, Franz. 2014. *The Trial* (David Wyllie trans.). New York: Dover Thrift Editions.

KANT, Immanuel. 1998. *Critique of Pure Reason* (Paul Guyer and Allen W. Wood eds and trans). Cambridge: Cambridge University Press.

——. 2008. *Universal Natural History and Theory of the Heavens, or An Essay on the Constitution and the Mechanical Origin of the Entire Structure of the Universe Based on Newtonian Principles* (Ian Johnston trans.). Arlington, VA: Richer Resources Publications.

KEATS, John. 1973a. *Endymion: A Poetic Romance* (1818) in *The Complete Poems*. London: Penguin, pp. 106–216.

———. 1973b. 'Why Did I Laugh Tonight?' (1818) in *The Complete Poems*. London: Penguin, p. 328.

KERÉNYI, Károly. 1977. *Görög mitológia*. Budapest: Gondolat.

———. 1983. 'Hérakleitos és a görög filozófia eredete' in Károly Kerényi and Kövendi Dénes (eds), *Hérakleitos múzsái vagy a természetről*. Budapest: Helikon Kiadó, pp. 42–68.

KIERKEGAARD, Søren. 1980. *The Concept of Anxiety* (Reidar Thomte trans.). Princeton, NJ: Princeton University Press.

KIRK, G. S. and J. E. Raven. 1957. *The Presocratic Philosophers: A Critical History with a Selection of Text*. Cambridge: Cambridge University Press.

KLAUSER, Theodor (ed.). 1981. *Reallexikon für Antike und Christentum*, VOL. 11. Stuttgart: Anton Hiersemann Verlag.

KLEIST, Heinrich von. 2013. 'On the Marionette Theatre' (Jean Wilson trans.) in Bert Cardullo (ed.), *Theories of the Avant-Garde Theatre: A Casebook from Kleist to Camus*. Lanham, MD: Scarecrow Press, pp. 41–8.

KOŁAKOWSKI, Leszek. 1988. *Metaphysical Horror* (Agnieszka Kolakowska trans.). Chicago: University of Chicago Press.

KÖLSCHER, U. 1968. 'Anaximander und die Anfänge der Philosophie' in Hans-Georg Gadamer (ed.), *Um die Begriffswelt der Vorsokratiker*. Darmstadt: Wissenschaftliche Buchgesellschaft, pp. 95–176.

LACAN, Jacques. 1978. *The Four Fundamental Concepts of Psycho-analysis* (Alan Sheridan trans.). New York: W. W. Norton.

LAUTRÉAMONT. 2011. *The Songs of Maldoror* (R. J. Dent trans.). Chicago: Solar Books / University of Chicago Press.

LEISEGANG, Hans. 1985. *Die Gnosis*. Stuttgart: Alfred Kröner Verlag.

LEVINAS, Emmanuel. 1996. 'The Poet's Vision' in *Proper Names* (Michael B. Smith trans.). Stanford, CA: Stanford University Press, pp. 127–39.

LIDDELL, H. D., and R. Scott. 1843. *Greek–English Lexicon*. Oxford: Clarendon Press.

LUCIAN. 1905. *Dialogues of the Gods* (H. W. and F. G. Fowler trans.). Oxford: Clarendon.

MACHO, Thomas H. 1993. 'Umsturz nach innen. Figuren der gnostischen Revolte' in Peter Sloterdijk and Thomas H. Macho (eds), *Weltrevolution der Seele*. Zürich: Artemis and Winkler, pp. 484–521.

MAHNKE, Dietrich. 1937. *Unendliche Sphäre und Allmittelpunkt*, Halle: Faksimile Neudruck der Ausg.

MAUS, Marcel. 1968. *Die Gabe*. Frankfurt am Main: Suhrkamp.

MEAD, G. R. S. 1896. *PISTIS SOPHIA: A Gnostic Miscellany; Being for the Most Part Extracts from the Books of the Saviour*. London: Theosophical Publishing Society.

———. 1906. *Fragments of a Faith Forgotten: Some Short Sketches among the Gnostics*. London: Theosophical Publishing Society.

MECHTILD OF MAGDEBURG. 1998. *The Flowing Light of the Godhead* (Frank Tobin trans.). New York: Paul List Press.

MELVILLE, Hermann. 1984. 'The Lightning-Rod Man' in *Pierre, Israel Potter, The Piazza Tales, The Confidence-Man, Billy Budd, and Uncollected Prose*. New York: Library of America, pp. 756–63.

MIŁOSZ, Czeslaw. 1985. *The Land of Ulro* (Louis Iribarne trans.). Manchester: Carcanet.

The 'Mithras' Liturgy from the Paris Codex. 1976. Marvin W. Meyer (trans.). Available at: https://goo.gl/3y3YpV (last accessed on 7 September 2016).

MUNDKUR, Balaji. 1983. *The Cult of the Serpent: An Interdisciplinary Survey of Its Manifestations and Origins*. Albany: State University of New York Press.

NEUMANN, Erich. 1955. *The Great Mother: An Analysis of the Archetype* (Ralph Manheim trans.). Princeton, NJ: Princeton University Press.

NIETZSCHE, Friedrich. 1974. *The Gay Science* (Walter Kaufmann trans.). London: Vintage Books.

———. 1980a. 'Die Geburt des tragischen Gedankens' in *Sämtliche Werke* (Giorgio Colli and Mazzino Montinari eds), VOL. 1. Munich: Deutscher Taschenbuch Verlag de Gruyter, pp. 579–600.

———. 1980b. 'Die Philosophie im tragischen Zeitalter der Griechen' in *Sämtliche Werke* (Giorgio Colli and Mazzino Montinari eds), VOL. 1. Munich: Deutscher Taschenbuch Verlag de Gruyter, pp. 799–872.

———. 1980c. 'Kommentar zur Kritischen Studienausgabe' in *Sämtliche Werke* (Giorgio Colli and Mazzino Montinari eds), VOL. 14. Munich: Deutscher Taschenbuch Verlag de Gruyter, pp. 87–138.

———. 1999. *Thus Spoke Zarathustra: A Book for All and None* (Thomas Common trans.). New York: Dover Thrift Editions.

———. 2006. *Thus Spoke Zarathustra: A Book for All and None* (Adrian del Caro trans.). Cambridge: Cambridge University Press.

NILSSON, M. P. 1961. *Geschichte der griechischen Religion*, 2 VOLS. Munich: C. H. Beck.

NORDEN, Eduard. 1913. *Agnostos theos. Untersuchungen zur Formengeschichte religiöser Reden*. Leipzig: Teubner.

OKEN, Lorenz. 1809. *Lehrbuch des Systems der Naturphilosophie*. Jena: Frommann.

OPPIAN. 1948. *Cynegetica* (A. W. Mair trans.). Loeb Classical Library. Cambridge, MA: Harvard University Press.

OTTO, Rudolf. 1936. *The Idea of the Holy* (John W. Harvey trans.). Oxford: Oxford University Press.

OVID. 1922. *Metamorphoses* (Brookes Moore trans.). Boston: Cornhill.

———. 1931. *Fasti* (James Fraser trans.). Loeb Classical Library. Cambridge, MA: Harvard University Press.

PARACELSUS, Theophrastus. 1968. *Magia naturalis* in *Werke*, VOL. 5 (Will-Erich Peuckert ed.). Basel and Stuttgart: Schwabe Verlag, pp. 53–377.

Paulys Realencyclopädie der classischen Altertumswissenschaft (RE). 1963. VOL. 24, HALF-VOL. 47. Stuttgart: Alfred Druckenmüller Verlag.

PAUSANIAS. 1954–55. *Description of Greece* (W. H. S. Jones and H. A. Ormerod trans). Loeb Classical Library. Cambridge, MA: Harvard University Press.

PENNICK, Nigel. 1979. *The Ancient Science of Geomancy*. London: Thames and Hudson.

PHILO OF ALEXANDRIA. 1993. *Who Is the Heir of Divine Things* in *The Works of Philo: Complete and Unabridged* (C. D. Yonge trans.). Peabody, MA: Hendrickson, pp. 276–303.

PHILOSTRATUS. 1912. *The Life of Apollonius of Tyana* (F. C. Conybeare trans.). Loeb Classical Library. Cambridge, MA: Harvard University Press.

Physiologus. 1979. Michael J. Curley (trans.). Chicago: University of Chicago Press.

PINDAR. 1990. *The Odes of Pindar* (Diane Arnson Svarlien trans.). Perseus Digital Library, Tufts University, MA. Available at: http://bit.ly/31WLQ8i (last accessed on 28 February 2017).

Pistis Sophia. 1905. In Carl Schmidt (ed.), *Koptisch-gnostische Schriften*, VOL. 1. Leipzig: Hinrich.

PISTORIUS, Hermann. 1785. *Einleitungsversuch über Aberglauben, Zauberey und Abgötterei*. Berlin.

PLATO. 1921a. *Sophist* in *Theaetetus. Sophist* (Harold North Fowler trans.). Loeb Classical Library. Cambridge, MA: Harvard University Press, pp. 259–460.

———. 1921b. *Theaetetus* in *Theaetetus. Sophist* (Harold North Fowler trans.). Loeb Classical Library. Cambridge, MA: Harvard University Press, pp. 1–258.

———. 1925. *Timaeus* (W. R. M. Lamb trans.). Cambridge, MA: Harvard University Press.

———. 1926a. *Laws* (R. G. Bury trans.), 2 VOLS. Loeb Classical Library. Cambridge, MA: Harvard University Press.

———. 1926b. *Parmenides* in *Cratylus. Parmenides. Greater Hippias. Lesser Hippias.* (Harold North Fowler trans.). Loeb Classical Library. Cambridge, MA: Harvard University Press, pp. 193–332.

———. 1929. *Epistles* in *Timaeus. Critias. Cleitophon. Menexenus. Epistles* (R. G. Bury trans.). Loeb Classical Library. Cambridge, MA: Harvard University Press, pp. 383–628.

———. 1935. *Republic* (Paul Shorey trans.), 2 VOLS. Cambridge, MA: Harvard University Press.

PLOTINUS. 1907–30. *The Six Enneads.* Stephen MacKenna and B. S. Page trans. Available at: https://www.sacred-texts.com/cla/plotenn/index.htm (last accessed on 1 March 2020).

PLUTARCH. 1919. *Alexander* in *Lives*, VOL. 7 (Bernadotte Perrin trans.). Loeb Classical Library. Cambridge, MA: Harvard University Press, pp. 223–440.

———. 1936a. *On the E at Delphi* in *Moralia*, VOL. 5 (Frank Cole Babbitt trans.). Loeb Classical Library. Cambridge, MA: Harvard University Press, pp. 192–253.

———.1936b. *Isis and Osiris* in *Moralia*, VOL. 5 (Frank Cole Babbitt trans.). Loeb Classical Library. Cambridge, MA: Harvard University Press, pp. 1–191.

POKORNY, Julius. 1959. *Indogermanisches Etymologisches Wörterbuch.* Bern and Munich: Francke Verlag.

PORPHYRY. 1920. *The Life of Pythagoras* (Kenneth Sylvan Guthrie trans.). Available at: http://bit.ly/2OXRPEJ (last accessed on 12 January 2020).

———. 2004. *On the Life of Plotinus and the Arrangement of His Work* (Stephen MacKenna trans.). Available at: http://bit.ly/38ysVDi (last accessed on 12 January 2020).

RAULFF, Ulrich. 1988. Afterword to Aby Warburg, *Schlangenritual. Ein Reisebericht.* Berlin: Klaus Wagenbach Verlag, pp. 63–94.

REINHARDT, Karl. 1977. *Parmenides.* Frankfurt am Main: Klostermann.

REUCHLIN, Johann. 1983. *On the Art of the Kabbalah (De Arte Cabalistica)* (Martin and Sarah Goodman trans). Lincoln: University of Nebraska Press.

RITTER, Joachim, and Karlfried Gründer (eds). 1971–84. *Historische Wörterbuch der Philosophie*, 13 VOLS. Basel and Stuttgart: Schwabe & Co. Verlag.

RORTY, Richard. 1991. *Essays on Heidegger and Others: Philosophical Papers.* Cambridge: Cambridge University Press.

ROSCHER, W. H. 1913. *Omphalos* in *Abhandlungen der Philologisch-historischen Klasse der Königlichen Sächsischen Gesellschaft der Wissenschaften*, VOL. 29, PART 9. Leipzig: B. G. Teubner.

ROSENZWEIG, Franz. 1985. *The Star of Redemption* (William W. Hallo trans.). Notre Dame, IN: University of Notre Dame Press.

SAINT-MARTIN, Louis-Claude de. 1979. *Le Crocodile ou la guerre du bien et du mal arrivée sous le règne de Louis XV. Poème epico-magigue (en prose).* Paris: Triades.

SCHELLING, F. W. J. 1856. *Sämmtliche Werke, Band 2: Philosophie der Mythologie.* Stuttgart and Augsburg: Cotta Verlag.

SCHLEIERMACHER, F. D. E. 1996[1988]. *On Religion: Speeches to Its Cultured Despisers* (Richard Crouter trans.). Cambridge: Cambridge University Press.

SCHMITT, E. H. 1903. *Die Gnosis. Grundlagen der Weltanschauung einer edleren Kultur*, 2 VOLS. Leipzig: Diederichs.

SCHOLEM, Gershom. 1990. *Origins of the Kabbalah* (R. J. Zwi Werblowski ed., Allan Arkush trans.). Princeton, NJ: Princeton University Press.

SCHRECKENBERG, Heinz. 1964. *Ananke: Untersuchungen zur Geschichte des Wortgebrauchs.* Munich: Beck.

SCHULTZ, Wolfgang. 1986. *Dokumente der Gnosis.* Munich: Matthes und Seitz.

SEABROOK, W. B. 1929. *The Magic Island.* London: George G. Harrap.

SHATTUCK, Roger. 1968. *The Banquet Years: The Origins of the Avant-Garde in France, 1885 to World War I.* New York: Vintage.

SILESIUS, Angelus. 1986. *The Cherubinic Wanderer* (Maria Shrady trans.). New York: Paulist Press.

SLOTERDIJK, Peter. 1993. *Weltfremdheit*. Frankfurt am Main: Suhrkamp Verlag.

SOPHOCLES. 1990. *Antigone* (Dudley Fitts and Robert Fitzgerald trans) in *Classical Tragedy: Greek and Roman*. New York: Applause Books, pp. 253–95.

SORABJI, Richard. 1983. *Time, Creation and the Continuum*. London: Duckworth.

STRABO. 2014. *The Geography of Strabo* (Duane W. Roller trans.). Cambridge: Cambridge University Press.

SUSO, Henry. 1989. *The Exemplar: With Two German Sermons* (Frank Tobin trans.). New York: Paulist Press.

TACITUS, Publius Cornelius. 1914. *Germania* in *Agricola, Germania, Dialogus* (Maurice Hutton and William Peterson trans; R. M. Ogilvie, E. H. Warmington and Michael Winterbottom revd). Loeb Classical Library. Cambridge, MA: Harvard University Press, pp. 128–217.

TAULER, Johannes. 1910. *The Sermons and Conferences of John Tauler* (Walter Elliott trans.). Washington, DC: Apostolic Mission House.

———. 2016. *Theologia Germanica* (Susanna Winkworth trans.). Scotts Valley, CA: Pantianos Classics.

UNAMUNO, Miguel de. 2000. *Mist* (Warner Fite trans.). Urbana and Chicago: University of Illinois Press.

USENER, Hermann. 1929. 'Bildung weiblicher Götternamen' in *Götternamen*. Bonn: Cohen Verlag, pp. 29–48.

VIRGIL. 2002. *Aeneid*. A. S. Kline (trans.). Available at: http://bit.ly/2SLNlSD (last accessed on 9 March 2017).

WACKENRODER, Wilhelm Heinrich. 1971. *Confessions and Fantasies* (Mary Hurst Schubert trans.). University Park: Pennsylvania State University Press.

WALKER, Barbara G. 1983. *The Women's Encyclopaedia of Myths and Secrets*. New York: Harper and Row.

WESTERINK, Leendert Gerrit. 1977. *The Greek Commentaries on Plato's 'Phaedo', Volume 2: Damascius*. Amsterdam: North Holland Publishing Company.